Interdisciplinary Understandings of Active Imagination

I0095036

Based on extensive research and developed with the support of the IAAP, this fascinating new work presents the precious value of the special legacy of C.G. Jung, which he himself defined as Active Imagination, through a collection of unpublished contributions by some of the brightest Jungian analysts and renowned representatives from the worlds of Art, Culture, Physics and Neurosciences.

In addition to presenting the genesis, development and results of Chiara Tozzi's research on Active Imagination, this volume explores the amplifications of Active Imagination in light of a range of disciplines. Contributors from all across the world give life to a multifaceted representation of this technique, showing the resonance that Active Imagination can have in the scientific, artistic and cultural fields, focussing on topics such as neuroscience, physics, literature, film, music, dance and painting.

Spanning two volumes, which are also accessible as standalone books, this essential collection will be of great interest to Jungian analysts, psychologists, psychoanalysts, or anyone interested in discovering more about the fascinating psychotherapeutic practice of Active Imagination and its interdisciplinary uses.

Chiara Tozzi is a Psychologist and Psychotherapist. She is a Training Analyst and Supervisor of *Associazione Italiana di Psicologia Analitica (AIPA)* and of the *International Association for Analytical Psychology (IAAP)*. She is also a Writer, Screenwriter and Screenwriting Professor. She is Artistic Director of the "*Mercurius Prize*", based in Zurich.

Interdisciplinary Understandings of Active Imagination

The Special Legacy of C.G. Jung

Edited by Chiara Tozzi

Routledge
Taylor & Francis Group
LONDON AND NEW YORK

Designed cover image: Getty Images

First published 2024
by Routledge
4 Park Square, Milton Park, Abingdon, Oxon OX14 4RN

and by Routledge
605 Third Avenue, New York, NY 10158

Routledge is an imprint of the Taylor & Francis Group, an informa business

British Library Cataloguing-in-Publication Data
A catalogue record for this book is available from the British
Library

ISBN: 978-1-032-53304-9 (hbk)
ISBN: 978-1-032-53302-5 (pbk)
ISBN: 978-1-003-41138-3 (ebk)

DOI: 10.4324/9781003411383

Typeset in Times New Roman
by Apex CoVantage, LLC

'This remarkable and exciting book brings C.G. Jung's Active Imagination to the creative, scientific, spiritual, and transdisciplinary needs of the twenty-first century. Perspicaciously rooted in Jung, the book reinvents the clinical and provides essential steppingstones for those taking this practice into art, philosophy and the synchronistic sciences. With this collection, Chiara Tozzi establishes herself as an important voice in analytical psychology and its multiple capacities to energize knowing and being.'

Susan Rowland

'This book offers a series of articles covering a wide scope with the aim of restoring Active Imagination to its rightful place as a significant method to access the unconscious and meaning in Jungian analysis. Active Imagination is a method developed by C.G. Jung which allowed him to access and delve into the images of his inner world and of the unconscious in order to more clearly understand their meaning and significance following the painful separation from Freud in 1913. The images and dialogues that emerged were recorded in the Red Book, which was kept private till its publication in 2019. The novelty of this method and the unusual images that emerged initially created concern in those around Jung and led some to question whether he was not falling into a state of psychosis. In fact, Jung was later very clear that it was precisely the use of Active Imagination and of the powerful images and dialogues that emerged as a result that enlightened him and led to a more profound understanding of the unconscious and of its archetypal contents. One of the legacies of the history of these early years is that there remains a lingering skepticism or mistrust with regard to the use and validity of Active Imagination. As a result, other than in training programs in Zurich, Active Imagination is often not given much attention. The editor of this book Chiara Tozzi sets out to address this lacuna and to restore Active Imagination to its rightful place as an invaluable avenue to access a living experience of psyche and of the unconscious in a personal manner. She manages this by bringing to the table, contributions from esteemed Jungian analysts who descrive their use of Active Imagination in clincial practice, which can include dialogues with dream figures, painting, meditation, body movement and dance. In addition, she has included voices from the world of the arts by inviting a director film/critic, a script writer, a professional dancer, a painter, an author, and a musician to reveal, from their unique and personal perspective, the central role that Active Imagination played in giving form to their creativity and of this method as a way of accessing the ephemeral from which meaning can emerge. The result is a wide-ranging collage of personal testimonies that attest to the usefulness of Active Imagination as a way to access the creative and the imaginal, in clinical practice, in their arts and in our daily lives as an avenue to find meaning. This book will appeal not only to analysts, therapists and artists but to everyone interested in their inner world and in creative expression. I highly recommend this book and am confident it will nourish many in their search for access to creativity and meaning in their lives.'

Tom Kelly

'The strength of this book lies in its rich tapestry of voices. It is impressive to learn about the applicability of Active Imagination in scientific, artistic, and cultural fields. The editor has masterfully gathered together an exceptional collaboration of authors that offers a multifaceted exploration of Active Imagination, providing readers with a treasure trove of insights and perspectives. Across the two volumes of this book, theory, practice, and research are assembled in a very creative way that includes research, methodology, theory and practice. Readers will find references to personal experiences and practical examples that help us understand the transformative power of Active Imagination as an indispensable attitude and tool in all creative processes and encounters with the unconscious. Real-life applications and personal anecdotes add depth and authenticity to this book. I am sure that Chiara Tozzi's two-volume book on *Active Imagination: Active Imagination in Theory, Practice and Training: The Special Legacy of C.G. Jung (vol 1) and Interdisciplinary Understandings of Active Imagination: The Special Legacy of C.G. Jung (vol 2)* is a significant contribution that keeps the spark alive of one of C.G. Jung's most important legacies.'

Pilar Amezaga

'Chiara Tozzi presents her research on the essential factor in analytical work that makes Jungians unique. Active Imagination is engagement with the psyche that speaks in images from within and from without. In this process one is guided by the wisdom of the Self that moves the development of the personality towards increased consciousness and wholeness. Tozzi clarifies that it is a process specific to the individual rather than a "technique". It furthers engagement with our fears and the unknown leading to the *Transcendent Function* that results in profound changes in our personality. Conversely though, it is this hard work and frightening engagement that deter many from its use. This book challenges us with a reminder of C.G. Jung's deeply effective creative path to healing.'

Nancy Swift Furlotti

To my masters,
to my patients,
to my students.

Contents

About the Editor

Chiara Tozzi is a Psychologist and Psychotherapist. She is a Training Analyst and Supervisor of *Associazione Italiana di Psicologia Analitica* (AIPA) and of the International Association for Analytical Psychology (IAAP). She is also a writer, screenwriter and screenwriting professor. She lectures internationally, and is a Visiting Professor to different IAAP Developing Groups. She is author of an International Research on Active Imagination supported by the IAAP, to be published by Routledge. She is Artistic Director of the international "Mercurius Prize for Films of Particular Psychological Significance and Sensitivity to Human Rights", based in Zurich. She is former editor of *Studi Junghiani*, the journal of the AIPA.

Contributors

Giacomo Aiolli is an Italian composer and producer based in Florence. He started his career playing in some local rock bands as a guitarist, then began to explore the world of electronic and computer music. He graduated from Conservatorio L. Cherubini in the "Music and New Technologies" department with a work called *Intro-Spettro* focused on the concepts of "synchronicity" theorized by C.G. Jung. *Intro-Spettro* is an open musical composition where a pseudo-random algorithm – inspired by Active Imagination and the I Ching's consultative method – decides the sound sequences to be selected.

He composed the soundtrack to Chiara Tozzi's documentary "The Lighting of Shadow Images – Interview with Giuseppe Tornatore", on Active Imagination, screened during the IAAP Conference "Film and Analytical Psychology", Belgrade, in May 2023.

With his band Zeronauta, he released an album in 2017 called *Controluce*, published by La Clinica Dischi. He often collaborates with solo artists and musical ensembles as producer and sound engineer. With his music, Aiolli wants to push himself towards unexplored sound environments and decode them through his music culture and sensibility, finding space to blend experimental and melodic sounds in a single composition.

Irene Cogliati Dezza is a research fellow in the Affective Brain Lab at University College London and Massachusetts Institute of Technology and in the CogComNeuroSci Lab at the University of Ghent. She is also associate editor for *In-Mind* magazine. She holds a BA in Biology, an MA in Neurobiology, a university certificate in data science, and a PhD in computational cognitive neuroscience. Cogliati Dezza's research focuses on information-seeking and exploration. In particular, she is interested in understanding how people decide what they want to know (information-seeking) and how they explore novel and unknown courses of action (exploration). In her research, she adopts state-of-the-art methods from different disciplines including psychology, neuroscience and computer science. She conducts her research in both healthy and psychiatric populations (i.e. addictive disorders, obsessive-compulsive disorders, attention deficit hyperactivity disorder, anxiety disorders).

Cogliati Dezza has gained several research grants and fellowships including two F.R.S-FNRS grants (2015, 2017, Belgium), the BOF post-doctoral fellowship (2019, Belgium) and the ULB Neuroscience Fellowship (2013, Belgium). Awards she has received include the CCN Student Travel Award (2018, USA), Excellent Student Award (2013, Italy), Post-master's degree Award (2013, Italy). She has published in peer-reviewed journals, including *Journal of Experimental Psychology: General* and *Nature Scientific Reports*. Her work has been selected for oral presentation at international conferences including the Belgium Association for Psychological Sciences Conference (2017, 2018) and Computational Cognitive Neuroscience (2018). She has organized several symposia at international conferences including an information-seeking symposium at the Cognitive Neuroscience Society 2020.

Umberto Contarello is a Scriptwriter, Writer and Actor. As a scriptwriter, he is especially known for the Oscar-awarded *The Great Beauty* (2013) by Paolo Sorrentino, *Io e te* (2012) by Bernardo Bertolucci, and *This Must Be the Place* (2011) by Paolo Sorrentino.

Ana Deligiannis is a Jungian Analyst, IAAP Member, Training and Supervising Analyst in the Training Program of Analytical Psychology, President of the Uruguayan-Argentinian Society for Analytical Psychology (SUAPA) – IAAP Group Member with Training Status. She is a psychotherapist specialized in Clinical Psychology (1977). She has a master's degree in Jungian Analytical Psychology-oriented Psychotherapy (Catholic University of Uruguay) and is Liaison Person of the Developing Group of Peru (APPA). She is: Founder Member, and Deputy Director, of the Argentine Association for Analytical Psychology (AsAPA) (2017–2020), and Founder Member of the Argentine Association for Dance Movement Therapy (AADT); Professor at the University of Buenos Aires (School of Medicine and Psychology), University of Belgrano, University of Flores, and University of Cordoba; Professor of the master's degree in Jungian Analytical Psychology at the Catholic University of Uruguay; Guest Professor at the Postgraduate in Dance-Movement Therapy at University CAECE. She was Director of the Teaching Area at the Center for Therapeutic Integration "Carl G. Jung" in Buenos Aires; Trainer of Trainers in Expressive Sandwork from the International Association for Expressive Sandwork (IAES); and has been Coordinator of the Sandwork projects in Argentina since 2013.

She is a lecturer in seminars and workshops in Colombia, Paraguay, Peru, Dominican Republic and Uruguay, as well as at national and international conferences. She has published articles in the *Journal of Analytical Psychology* and chapters in books (Ed. Kohlhammer y Prensa Médica Latinoamericana). Preface and coordination of the edition project of the book by Eva Pattis Zoja: *Expressive Sandwork in Vulnerable Populations. A Jungian Approach* (Spanish Edition) Buenos Aires: Published by Letra Viva (2016).

She is also a contemporary dancer and integrates the experience of the body and movement into the psychotherapeutic area. She works with Movement as

Active Imagination in individual and group sessions. She has a private practice in Buenos Aires, Argentina.

Karin Fleischer is an IAAP Jungian Analyst, Training and Supervising Analyst, professional Member of the Uruguayan-Argentinian Society for Analytical Psychology (SUAPA). She is on the Executive Board (2018–2021) of the Latin American Committee for Analytical Psychology (CLAPA). She is a licensed Psychologist (Buenos Aires University) and holds a master's degree in Dance Movement Therapy (California State University, East Bay, USA). She is a founder Member of SUAPA and of the Argentinian Association of Dance Movement Therapy (AADT). Co-director of a Master Program in Dance Movement Therapy at the University of Arts (Buenos Aires) and University Professor in graduate and post-graduate courses in Analytical Psychology at various national Universities. She has introduced Authentic Movement/Active Imagination in movement, in Argentina and in several Latin American countries, teaching seminars on the Body and Active Imagination, nationally and internationally, during the past 25 years. Her article, "The Symbol in the Body: The Undoing of a Dissociation through Embodied Active Imagination in Jungian Analysis", was published by the *Journal of Analytical Psychology*, in June 2020. She is currently interested in exploring the importance of symbolic somatic approaches, as Authentic Movement, bridging implicit and explicit narratives in the clinical treatment of trauma and attachment disorders. She has a private practice in Buenos Aires.

Margarita Méndez is an IAAP Training and Supervising Analyst in Venezuela and internationally. Her contributions grow from her twin roots in archetypal psychology and contemporary dance. She acknowledges the body as a resource in Jungian analysis and has applied its many uses in attempting resolution of personal, social and political conflicts. Her passion lies in the possible integration of body, psyche and the creative/healing potentials of the unconscious *via* Active Imagination. She was the Director of Studies of the Venezuelan Society of Jungian Analysts (SVAJ) from 2009–2012, and Convener from 2011–2013 and 2018–2020. She is interested in incorporating the psychic body in Jungian Analysis in her private practice, articles and talks.

Through the teachings of her mentor Rafael López-Pedraza, she has explored three mythic experiences of the body from the antique Greek tradition: *Pan* son of Hermes, *Psyche*'s psychic living body and *Dionysus*, the body. These images may invite others' inner myths to arise, so clients are free to choose or be chosen by a different image or experience. It is essential to stay with and hold what the psyche first brings into our bodies, so we may enter into it through dance/movement; first, with our individual selves, and then explore interaction between us and others while working in groups.

Gianfranca Nieddu, MD, PhD, is a Psychiatrist and expert at the court of Sassari. Since 2020, she has been a Jungian Analyst and IAAP and AIPA Member. She works in the Department of Mental Health and Addictions of Sassari. She is an expert in Diagnosis and Therapy of Eating Disorders. She was Coordinator of several rehabilitation projects in the field of mental health, in collaboration with theater companies. She is co-author of several scientific papers on the subject of interest including publications, posters and conference reports. She attended the AIPA Training Seminar on Active Imagination by Chiara Tozzi in 2019 and was a speaker at the conference on Active Imagination by Chiara Tozzi: "Who Is Afraid of Active Imagination?" (AIPA, Rome 2019) as well as the seminar by Chiara Tozzi "From Horror to Ethical Responsibility" (AIPA, Milan 2020). She participated with an audiovisual contribution to the "Open Day" (AIPA, Rome, 2020).

Her video *Passavamo sulla terra leggeri . . .* was screened at the opening of the International Conference "Psyche and Environment" organized by Chiara Tozzi in collaboration with AIPA, CIPA, ARPA, Rome, 2019 (guest and speaker: IAAP President Prof. Toshio Kawai). She lives in Italy and has a private practice in Sassari.

Luca Padroni is a contemporary Italian artist known for his large-scale works in which fields of color form different architectural spaces. The starting point in his work is drawings and small-scale studies in oil which evolve into monumental paintings. Powerful and ambiguous, his paintings embrace the observer as an integral part of the image. The formal composition of his pictures depicts a vigorous sense of motion, through the creation of unrealistic and impossible architecture of spaces, he reveals his fascinating perception of the surrounding world.

Having spent most of his childhood and adolescence in various African countries, including South Africa, the artist has developed a special fascination for nature and the animal world, now threatened more than ever before. The latest Jungle series is an attempt by the artist to communicate and remember where we come from, our ancestors' identity, our indissoluble bond to nature.

Padroni has taken part in numerous solo and group exhibitions in Italy and abroad. Among those recently held at Public Institutions: *Summer Exhibition*, curated by Timothy Hyman, Royal Academy, London (2019); *Scorribanda*, curated by Fabio Sargentini, Galleria Nazionale di Arte Moderna e Contemporanea, Rome (2018); *I Valori Personali*, curated by Claudio Crescentini, Pad. 9b Macro Testaccio, Rome (2017).

Elsa Piperno is a dancer, choreographer, "pioneer of contemporary dance in Italy" as she has often been called. She began her studies at the Italian National Dance Academy, moving to London to study at the Marie Rambert School, and in the 1960s she was part of the building block which, in 1967, became the "London Contemporary Dance Theatre" (LCDT), a well-known company directed by Robert Cohan. As a solo dancer with the LCDT she also had the opportunity to work and study with leading exponents of the main strands of American *modern dance* (techniques and repertoire of José Limòn, Alwin Nikolais, Merce Cunningham, Paul Taylor).

At the beginning of the 1970s she left the LCDT and moved back to Rome where she founded and directed the dance school "Centro Professionale di Danza Contemporanea" and then the dance company "Teatrodanza Contemporanea di Roma", which she directed with Robert Curtis and then Joseph Fontano until its closure in 1989. In 1990, she founded a new company, "Danzare la vita".

She has also created choreographies for cinema.

Her choreographies have been performed in major theaters and festivals in Italy and internationally.

From her earliest days in the LCDT she displayed a distinct talent for teaching dance. She was personally selected by Robert Cohan to spread the knowledge and practice of Graham-based modern dance technique throughout the United Kingdom and abroad. In England, she has taught at: The Laban Art of Movement Guild; Sussex University; Guildford School of Dance; University of Durham; Dartington College of Arts. In Italy, she has taught at: Teatro Comunale in Florence; Teatro Municipale Romolo Valli di Reggio Emilia; Teatro dell'Opera di Roma; Sapienza University of Rome; Università di Bologna DAMS. Internationally, she has taught at: Centre International de la Dance in Paris; Ballettakademien, Statendanskola, Birgit Cullberg Studio, Royal Swedish Ballet in Stockholm; l'Institute Superieur d'Art Drammatique in Rabat (Morocco); Instituto Nacional Superior del Profesorado de danza, Asociacion Arte y Cultura, I Festival De Danza Del Mercosur, Dirección Nacional De Musica y Danza, Ballet Folclorico Nacional in Buenos Aires (Argentina); International Dance Summer School in Komiza (Croatia). She held the Chair in Modern Dance Technique at the Italian National Academy of Dance where she taught from the early 1980s until 2012.

Emiliano Puddu is Professor of Fundamentals of Physics at the University Cattaneo LIUC in Castellanza (Varese). After graduating in physics, he carried out research in the field of nonlinear optics, applied to holography and imaging, which resulted in 20 academic publications.

He lives in Como. Alongside his work as a physics professor, Prof. Puddu has always kept alive his passions, devoting himself mainly to Jungian psychology, painting and classical culture.

Mario Sesti is a Director, Film Critic and Journalist. He has directed more than ten documentary films, all broadcast by free and pay tv and selected by Cannes, Venice, Locarno and screened at the MoMA and at the Guggenheim in New York. He won the prize for the best film book twice (in 1994 with *Nuovo Cinema Italiano* and in 1997 with *Tutti i film* di Pietro Germi) and in 2005 the Diego Fabbri Award for the best film-book of the year with *In quel film c'è un segreto*.

He is one of the curators of the Rome Film Festival. From 2012 to 2014, he directed the Taormina Film Fest. He wrote and directed, among others, films about Pasolini (*La voce di Pasolini*, 2005, together with Matteo Cerami) and Fellini (*L'ultima sequenza*, 2003, selected by Cannes Film Festival). In 2019,

Cannes Film Festival selected his film about Bernardo Bertolucci (*No End Travelling*) and Venice Film Festival selected *Mondo Sexy*, about Italian erotic documentaries in the 1960s.

Dario Voltolini is a Writer, Journalist, Lyricist, Librettist, and Author of radio plays. He has published with many Italian publishers including Einaudi, Feltrinelli, Mondadori, La Nave di Teseo and Bollati Boringhieri. He is former professor and director of the "Holden School of Storytelling & Performing Arts". He has collaborated with the newspapers La Stampa and La Repubblica, written many radio plays for RAI Radiotelevisione Italiana, and many lyrics for songs and musical theater. He is a correspondent from Italy for "OGGI7", the Sunday insert of the American newspaper AmericaOggi. He is Creator of Ecological Niche DietTM, and Co-Founder, Treasurer, and Press Officer of the "Lorenzo Bracco Foundation".

Chapter 1

Active Imagination
The Special Legacy of C.G. Jung

Chiara Tozzi

The Pursuit of Active Imagination

The objective of this two-volume book on active imagination can be defined by two statements by C.G. Jung. I will begin with the first:

> The years when I was pursuing my inner images were the most important in my life – in them everything essential was decided. It all began then; the later details are only supplements and clarifications of the material that burst forth from the unconscious, and at first swamped me. It was the prima materia for a lifetime's work.
>
> (Jung, 1961, MDR, cap. VI p. 137)

When I read *Memories, Dreams, Reflections* for the first time in 1978, it was this very sentence, and the account of C.G. Jung's courageous confrontation with the unconscious, that particularly struck me. In the description of that dialogue and encounter with obscure and dangerous parts of oneself, which could fascinate but also instill horror, I found echoed the significant contents and images of the fairytales and legends that had captivated me as much as any other kid in childhood, regardless of the time and space in which that narration had taken place. And it was exactly from listening to and reading fairytales that a passion for storytelling was born in me, both as a mode of communication and as a profession, in literature and film.

When I started my training to become a Jungian analyst at Associazione Italiana di Psicologia Analitica (AIPA) in 1996, Dr Bianca Garufi, one of the most important Italian Jungian analysts, explained to me that this way of confronting the unconscious, first experimented by Jung on himself, was a real form of therapy, specific to Jungian clinical practice and referred to as active imagination.

Meeting Bianca Garufi resulted in a friendship that was precious to me. I met her at the making of the feature film *Le parole sono altrove*[1] (Tozzi *et al.*, 2000) with the AIPA Cinema Group. Bianca Garufi – with whom I had carried out one of the interviews needed to be admitted to the AIPA-IAAP Training – was the one who had invited me to join the AIPA Cinema Group because, although I was

DOI: 10.4324/9781003411383-1

then an AIPA trainee and not yet an AIPA-IAAP member, I had been a scriptwriter and screenplay teacher for over a decade. Bianca Garufi, in addition to being an AIPA-IAAP training analyst, was a recognized writer and poet: as a writer, she had published several books, including a novel written in four hands, including one of the most important Italian writers, Cesare Pavese (Garufi and Pavese, 1959). Here, I would like to recall one of her qualities as a poet – as I have done elsewhere: her splendid poem "Non l'Io" (Not the Ego; Garufi, 2002), referring precisely to the conversation between the Ego and the unconscious that takes place during the experience of active imagination. I was thus fortunate to have a first illustration of the complex and special essence of active imagination precisely through that "double-meaning" language that Bianca Garufi used spontaneously, and of which Jung speaks about his way of writing (von Franz, 1988): i.e. giving voice to a harmonious interaction between consciousness and the unconscious. Bianca Garufi, as an artist, could express herself and write in such a special way because she naturally possessed that more permeable diaphragm between consciousness and the unconscious (Jung, 1916/58), which for Jung is typical of creative people; yet, that more permeable diaphragm can be reached by anyone through the experience of active imagination, by virtue of the activation of the transcendent function, that is, that "movement out of the suspension between two opposites, a living birth that leads to a new level of being, a new situation" (Jung, 1916/58, par. 189).

The specificity of the therapeutic method Jung had identified and experimented on himself, i.e. active imagination, seemed to me extraordinary and valuable; at the same time, the fact that, during the six years of AIPA training and afterwards, I heard very little about it in the Jungian community was disconcerting.

Over time, I learned that this bizarre scotomization of a legacy that appears to be not only precious, but Jung's most specific clinical methodology compared with other psychoanalytical methods developed by famous scholars of the psyche, was not only taking place in Italy, but throughout the international Jungian community. Certainly, the publication of *The Red Book* (Jung, 2009) and its worldwide dissemination necessarily led to recognizing that "first matter for a lifetime's work" mentioned by Jung in *Memories, Dreams, Reflections*. But what else was that "first matter," so admirably depicted and described in *The Red Book*, if not precisely the contents of the unconscious that sprang from Jung's courageous experience of active imagination? And yet, while such contents and illustrations, after the publication of *The Red Book* by Sonu Shamdasani, became the object of in-depth study by the international Jungian community and anyone interested in the psyche, the same cannot be said for the dissemination of active imagination, which was also at the origin of those contents and illustrations. Focusing on one of the special qualities of *The Red Book*, namely its ability to symbolically illustrate a complex psychological journey through written and visual images that were never saturated, I decided to refer precisely to that double background used by Jung to explain his expository peculiarity. I therefore made a video, entitled *Un doppio fondo*,[2] in which I tried to summarize the affinities between the language of film and those of C.G. Jung's analytical psychology.

Encouraged by the feedback I received from some IAAP colleagues,[3] I continued to explore this connection between languages in light of active imagination, and followed up the screening of the video (the English version is called *En Route*) for the paper "En Route: From Active Imagination to Film Language," which I presented in 2013 at the 19th IAAP International Congress in Copenhagen (Tozzi, 2014).

After becoming a training analyst, in 2014 I was given the Seminar on active imagination at AIPA, which I have held every year since then (Colangeli, 2022). My first concern at the time was to try to pass on to AIPA trainees not only the theoretical aspect of active imagination, but what Jung had truly tried to pass on to us with his personal experience. In fact, I believe Jung does not *reductively and literally* tell us that what he wants to pass on and deliver is a pattern, a technique, or a method; rather, he leaves us a personal and suffered testimony, experienced first-hand, on *how* he symbolically lived the years when he practiced active imagination. His reluctance to present a "technical" pattern and outline of the practice of active imagination shows us how important it is to leave more space in the life of human beings for the individuative and transformative meaning and outcome of active imagination, as seen in *Memories, Dreams, Reflections* and in *The Red Book*.

Actually, I had and still have the impression there is a twofold approach within the Jungian community to the possibility of learning and teaching active imagination (Tozzi, 2023):

1 as a mainly mentalized repetition of a technique;
2 as a personalized integration of a different way of being in the world, of a capacity for equal confrontation with the unconscious, related to synchronicity and fundamental in the process of *individuation*.

The first and meaningful support to represent the approach I believed is most in line with the meaning given by Jung of active imagination (that is, the second one) came to me from Gerhard Adler's description of active imagination, in *Studies in Analytical Psychology* (Adler, 1948). In that essay, Gerhard Adler very efficiently clarifies the difference between the two approaches, arguing that one cannot speak of a

> "technique" of active imagination just as one can hardly speak of a "technique of dreaming" [. . .] By "active imagination" we understand a *definite attitude* towards the contents of the unconscious [. . .] The right attitude may perhaps be best described as one of "active passivity" [. . .] It is not unlike watching a film or listening to music [. . .] Only the difference is that in active imagination the "film" is being unrolled inside.
>
> (Adler, 1948, pp. 56–57)

To me, this brilliant and evocative explanation, based both on logic and on the metaphorical use of images, translated into a further image: that of "a different way of being in the world" (Tozzi, 2017), reachable through the individuative experience in active imagination. Based on this assumption, I decided to submit a proposal for the 20th IAAP International Congress to be held in Tokyo, Japan, in 2016. Before the Congress in Kyoto, a second contribution was fundamental to convince me that the journey I had embarked on in my research on active imagination truly made sense. As I have broadly described elsewhere (Tozzi, 2023, op. cit.), in the summer of 2015 I was at Yale University[4] to present "The Experience of Grace: The Possibility of Transformation in Vladimir Nabokov and Carl Gustav Jung" (Tozzi, 2015). There, I attended Murray Stein's incredible conference, "Synchronizing Time and Eternity: A Matter of Practice" (Stein, 2017). On that occasion, Stein's presentation was unfolding all my doubts and dilemmas related to my choice to teach, practice, and experience active imagination as an *attitude* and not as a *technique*. Actually, in his lecture, Stein presented an active imagination done by Pauli in 1953, stimulated by Jung and M.L. von Franz and defined by Pauli himself as "The Piano Lesson." In "The Piano Lesson," Pauli questioned himself on the same dilemma I was facing, represented in his active imagination, as follows: "There were two schools: in the older of the two one understood words but not meaning, while in the newer one understood meaning but not my words. I could not bring the two schools together" (Atmanspacher, Primus, and Wertenschlag-Birkhauser, 1995, pp. 317–330). Stein explained the two positions as follows:

At one level, this is a reference to the schools of nuclear physics and analytical psychology; at another level, it refers to the explanations that science offers and the meanings that derive from a depth psychological and spiritual orientation. Here Pauli was stuck.

(Stein, op. cit. p. 50)

As highlighted by Stein, to metaphorically represent this situation:

What he [Pauli, Ed.] came up with was a marvelous image, the piano, which with its black and white keys resonates with the Chinese yang-yin system. [. . .] But then it became a matter of learning "to play the piano," not only of understanding the issues intellectually [. . .]. This was the challenge put to him by Jung and von Franz.

(Stein, op. cit., p. 50)

After sharing Pauli's touching and meaningful active imagination, Stein added:

Pauli faces this issue head-on in this "active fantasy." The piano symbolizes a possible point of meeting. It represents the transcendent function, a synthetic mind. Of course, the question is: Can he play the piano? Well, he is learning. [. . .] At any rate, Pauli has given us in the image of the piano a useful metaphor for the transcendent function, which may assist our efforts to create a sustained and sustaining link between time and eternity for ourselves and with our patients.

(Stein, op. cit., pp. 55–56)

Following this inspiring lecture, when I was back in Rome I decided to write to Murray Stein, although I did not know him personally. I told him how much I had appreciated his lecture at Yale and I explained to him that, by presenting Pauli's active imagination on "The Piano Lesson," he had given a symbolic answer to my consideration on the two ways of experiencing and passing on active imagination. After all, my question on how to explain an attitude of active imagination had already been answered in the title of his lecture: it is . . . "A matter of practice"!

Ever since, all my detailed studies, conferences, and seminars on active imagination have been focused on trying to pass on to colleagues, patients, and trainees the meaning of that "different way of being in the world," given by a true experience of active imagination, as well as by the fascinating connections between active imagination and other forms of expression and of human research.

But . . . there is a but!

As I felt the enthusiasm and interest grow within me and received positive feedback on active imagination from many IAAP colleagues and trainees, both in Italy and in other countries I was visiting regularly as IAAP Visiting Professor, the dissemination and formation on this special Jungian method was still lacking.

When trainees asked me for a bibliography, I was forced to note there was a clear lack of publications in the field, especially compared with other topics that are more followed and analyzed within the Jungian community. I asked myself the reason for this scotomization, so unequal compared to such unique magnificence which we possess as Jung's followers. I came up with a possible answer: that, in fact, active imagination . . . scares. Nothing weird about that, considering the complex and delicate journey to undergo to reach a dialogue with the unconscious in a waking state, as required by active imagination. Yet, although understandable in patients and trainees, such blind fear is not comprehensible in Jungian analysts and, actually, seemed to me to be quite concerning. This is how I came up with the idea of addressing this "troublesome" issue at the 21st IAAP International Congress to be held in Vienna. I submitted my proposal of this difficult topic and I am thankful to my IAAP colleagues not only for accepting my presentation, but for inviting me to present "From Horror to Ethical Responsibility: Carl Gustav Jung and Stephen King Encounter the Dark Half Within Us, Between Us and in the World" in a plenary session. I must say that the unexpected and enthusiastic reaction by colleagues on that occasion was an additional stimulus that pushed me to go full throttle and even more in-depth: I ventured into a collective research on active imagination that I could have presented to IAAP colleagues. My video-interview, "The Lighting of Shadow Images – Interview with Giuseppe Tornatore,"[5] shot in the projection room of Tornatore's office in August 2019, in which Oscar-awarded director Giuseppe Tornatore confronts himself with Jungian active imagination for the first time, was another important step that pushed me to carry on with my project.

The final spark came from something else, but I will talk about that at the end of this chapter.

Support and Cooperation for My International Research on Active Imagination

This book is therefore the result of my research on active imagination, carried out with the support of the IAAP.

My proposal was submitted to the IAAP Academic Sub-Committee in 2021, and was soon after approved and granted a fund.[6]

In my research project, I asked for, and received, the collaboration of many IAAP colleague analysts from different countries who were particularly interested and who specialized in active imagination. I also asked for, and received, contributions from experts in the worlds of Neurosciences, Physics, Art, and Culture. The Research Unit RISORSA – Social Research, Organization and Risk in Health – of DiSSE – Department of Social and Economic Sciences – of the Sapienza University of Rome, Italy also provided their collaboration.

Additional support was also given by Shannon Marie Clay, freelance interpreter and translator who supported me in editing the book and translating some of the chapters. I am really thankful to Shannon, the backbone of this entire journey.

Following, the final list of participants:

IAAP Analysts

1   Tozzi, Chiara, AIPA-IAAP, Italy
2   Adorisio, Antonella, CIPA- IAAP, Italy
3   Bonasera, Gaetana, AIPA-IAAP, Italy
4   Cassar, Laner, Malta Jung Developing Group-IAAP, Malta
5   Colangeli, Valerio, AIPA-IAAP, Italy
6   De Luca Comandini, Federico, AIPA-IAAP, Italy
7   Deligiannis, Ana, SUAPA-IAAP, Argentina
8   Fleischer, Karin, SUAPA, IAAP, Argentina
9   Méndez, Margarita, SVAJ-IAAP, Venezuela
10 Mercurio, Robert, ARPA, Italy[7]
11 Nieddu, Gianfranca, AIPA-IAAP, Italy
12 Pattis Zoja, Eva, CIPA, Italy
13 Renn, Regina, DGAP- IAAP, Germany[8]
14 Stein, Murray, AGAP-IAAP, Switzerland
15 Tibaldi, Marta, AIPA-IAAP, Italy

Representatives from the Worlds of Art, Culture, Neurosciences, and Physics, and Sapienza University of Rome, Italy

16 Aiolli, Giacomo, musician, Italy
17 Clay, Shannon Marie, linguist, Italy

18 Cogliati Dezza, Irene, research fellow in the Affective Brain Lab at University College London and Massachusetts Institute of Technology
19 Contarello, Umberto, scriptwriter, Italy
20 Padroni, Luca, painter, Italy
21 Piperno, Elsa, dancer, choreographer and dance teacher, Italy
22 Puddu, Emiliano, physics professor, Italy
23 Sesti, Mario, critic-journalist, Film Festival Director and Documentary Director, Italy
24 Voltolini, Dario, writer, Italy
25 Research Unit RISORSA – Social Research, Organization and Risk in Health – of DiSSE – Department of Social and Economic Sciences – of the Sapienza University of Rome, Italy[9]

Research Characteristics and Methodology

First Phase

My research on active imagination was a "qualitative" research which therefore required the necessary tools to translate qualitative data into quantitative data for the needed analysis and comparisons.

To this end, two "structured" questionnaires with predefined answers were provided for a numerical translation. One questionnaire was sent to IAAP members, trainees, and routers to verify their knowledge, appreciation, and clinical practice of active imagination. A second questionnaire was sent to the people in charge of IAAP training (IAAP training analysts) and covered the relevance given to active imagination during IAAP trainings.

The questionnaires were submitted through an online platform and, based on the answers received, were processed in progress by the Research Unit RISORSA of Sapienza University of Rome, Italy.

A report on the answers collected was sent to me, and I then forwarded the results to my IAAP colleagues who contributed to this research.

The results of the first phase were aimed at providing useful material for a personal processing and/or a collective discussion among IAAP analysts taking part in this research. The material was made available for analysts to use in their personal contributions to the research.

Second Phase

During the second phase, the IAAP analysts working on this research were free to choose whether they wanted to work by themselves on a topic related to active imagination, or to exchange opinions with myself and/or the other participants.

At the same time, during the second phase, additional contributions were provided by a neuroscientist and a physics professor, as well as contributions and amplifications from the world of contemporary culture and art.

The results of the questionnaires and the contributions and knowledge provided by participants could be shared collectively after I sent them out. This was aimed at favoring a network of connection and exchange among IAAP analysts taking part in the research, and among the neuroscientist and physics professor and all representatives from the world of culture and arts who decided to take part in this specific research development. This exchange could lead to further contributions aimed at providing detailed empirical studies as well as new and original content to corroborate the importance given by C.G. Jung to active imagination. Moreover, it could help to highlight that active imagination is a unique psychotherapeutic method, different from all the other methods available and practiced in psychoanalysis and psychotherapy.

The results of the research were collected in a structured database. From the beginning, a possible outcome of such data and all material produced and collected was to give life to a publication managed by me, as editor of this research.

The quality of the questionnaire was monitored by the Research Unit RISORSA of Sapienza University of Rome. I then analyzed the results of the questionnaire and summarized and interpreted them.

Trend of the Research

The research project started in 2021, stemming from the hypothesis that the theory and practice of active imagination, although fundamental and crucial in C.G. Jung's analytical psychology, are not well known, studied, and practiced within the Jungian community, and are very little known to all those who are not part of the purely psychoanalytical setting.

The first goal of my research was to:

1 Verify the truthfulness of the hypothesis through one questionnaire divided in two parts, as previously described. I designed and then prepared and managed the questionnaire with the support of the Research Unit RISORSA, DiSSE, Department of Social and Economic Sciences of Sapienza University of Rome, Italy.

The questionnaire was to be sent to all IAAP members, routers, and trainees, and IAAP training analysts.

Questionnaire Emerging Questions

i How aware are IAAP members of active imagination?
ii Was active imagination considered meaningful and valuable in C.G. Jung's clinical practice?
iii How much importance is given by IAAP members to active imagination as a psychotherapeutic method?
iv Which scientific, artistic, and expressive fields can be linked to active imagination?

   v   To what level is active imagination used in Jungian psychotherapy?
   vi How much research is there on active imagination?
   vii Is active imagination properly addressed in IAAP training?
   viii How to bridge the possible gap at the level of training, knowledge, and clinical practice?

2 Analyze and evaluate the results of the questionnaires.
3 Prepare a database based on the scientific evidence of the theoretical knowledge, practice, and training of active imagination by IAAP analysts to support IAAP dissemination programs about active imagination at the international level.

Administration, Timing of Data Processing, and Validity of the Questionnaire

The questionnaire was carried out and processed by the Research Unit RISORSA – Social Research, Organization and Risk in Health – of DiSSE – Department of Social and Economic Sciences – of the Sapienza University of Rome, Italy

The survey was carried out from August 27 to October 15, 2021.

The questionnaires were sent by the IAAP Secretariat to 3,564 individuals among IAAP training analysts and IAAP members, and to 378 individuals among IAAP routers and trainees, for a total of 3,942 individuals.

Overall, 12.63 percent of the reference population answered the questionnaires.

The level of response was sufficient for an online survey and it could therefore be considered valid.

Interpretation of the Final Data of the Questionnaire

First consideration: although the questionnaire is valid, I think it is interesting to think about this: why didn't 87.37 percent – almost 90 percent! – of IAAP members respond to the questionnaire?

Only in a few countries was there a high response rate to the questionnaire. Among these, for IAAP members, routers, and trainees the highest response was recorded in:

United States	87
China	27
Italy	27
United Kingdom	24

For IAAP training analysts, the highest response was recorded in:

Germany	38
United States	27
Switzerland	17

Total Respondents by Country

COUNTRY	N	COUNTRY	N
Argentina	4	Italy	27
Australia	2	Japan	3
Austria	4	Latvia and Lithuania	1
Belarus	2	Lithuania	1
Belgium	3	Luxembourg	1
Brazil	23	Malta	3
Bulgaria	3	Mexico	2
Canada	12	Netherland	1
Chile	2	Peru	1
China	27	Poland	2
Colombia	1	Portugal	1
Czech republic	1	Romania	5
Denmark	5	Russia	11
Dominican Republic	2	Serbia	3
Estonia	1	South Africa	5
France	8	South Korea	3
Georgia	11	Spain	4
Germany	9	Switzerland	18
Hong Kong	1	UK	24
Hungary	1	Ukraine	6
India	5	Uruguay	2
International	1	USA	87
Ireland	1	Venezuela	2
Israel	2	**Total overall**	**344**

Figure 1 Table of IAAP member, router, and trainee respondents by country.

Total Respondents by Country

COUNTRY	N
Argentina	2
Australia	2
Austria	4
Brazil	8
Canada	5
Chile	1
China	3
Czech republic and the Netherlands	1
Denmark	3
Deutschland, schweiz	1
France	4
Germany	38
Israel	10
Italy	13
Italy and Switzerland	1
Japan	1
Russia	3
Serbia	1
South Africa	1
South Korea	1
Spain	2
Switzerland	17
UK	4
Uruguay	1
USA	27
Total overall	**154**

Figure 2 Table of IAAP training analyst respondents by country.

The first interesting result is seen in Germany, where only nine IAAP members, routers, and trainees answered the questionnaire (resulting among the lowest countries per response rate), while there was a high response rate among IAAP training analysts, accounting for 38 respondents and therefore positioning itself at the top of the list. This is an inverted trend compared with the rest of the countries, where there was a lower response rate among IAAP training analysts than among IAAP members, routers, and trainees. It is true that there are fewer IAAP training analysts than IAAP members, routers, and trainees in the different IAAP Associations, but it would be interesting to assess the results of the high or low number of training analysts who participated in the questionnaire. For example, in Italy, among all AIPA, CIPA, and ARPA training analysts – that is, 305 individuals – only 13 answered the questionnaire, accounting for 4.2 percent of all Italian IAAP training analysts. It may be useful and interesting for IAAP Associations in the different countries to calculate *ex-post* the percentage of training analysts who answered the questionnaire in each country.

Considering the results presented above, it appears that although IAAP members, routers, and trainees, and IAAP training analysts consider active imagination to be a meaningful component for C.G. Jung (95.3 percent and 90 percent, respectively) both at theoretical and clinical level, they are not adequately informed about such practice.

QUESTION: In your opinion, did C. G. Jung consider
Active Imagination to be meaningful and
valuable in his clinical practice?

Overall:

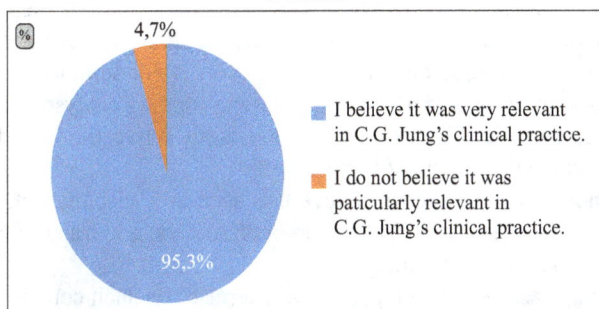

Figure 3 Percentage of IAAP member, router, and trainee respondents who believe and who do not believe C.G. Jung considered active imagination to be meaningful and valuable in his clinical practice.

Among those who answered the questionnaire, only 48.7 percent of IAAP training analysts experienced active imagination as patients, 69 percent experienced it in training, and yet 81.9 percent use it in their clinical practice, showing that a large number of IAAP training analysts use active imagination even though they may not have personally experienced it during their analysis. This leads to a first interesting question: since many IAAP training analysts use the practice of active imagination without having experienced it as patients or trainees, are we truly able to provide the skills necessary to use active imagination in our clinical practice? Are we sufficiently trained to pass on the knowledge and practice of active imagination to IAAP trainees?

*QUESTION: In your opinion, did C. G. Jung consider Active Imagination
to be meaningful and valuable in his clinical practice?*

Overall:

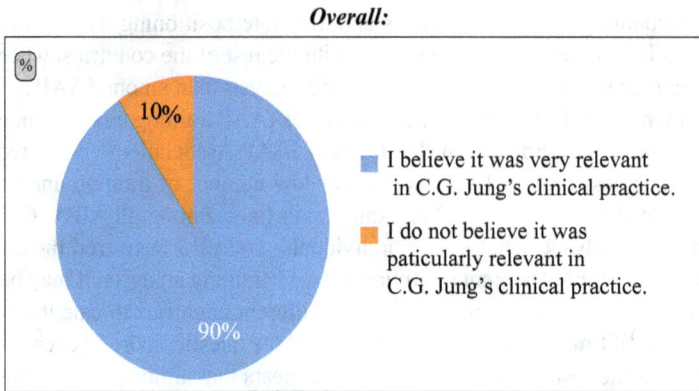

Figure 4 Percentage of IAAP training analyst respondents who believe and who
do not believe C.G. Jung considered active imagination to be meaningful
and valuable in his clinical practice.

Only 38.1 percent and 36.3 percent of all members, routers, and trainees are
familiar with the scientific literature on active imagination in international journals and in their country's accredited journals of analytical psychology. For IAAP
training analysts, the percentages account for 54 percent and 50.6 percent, leading
us to think there may be a lack of stimuli on the subject. This seems to once again
confirm that the knowledge on active imagination is not sufficiently widespread
among members, routers, and trainees, nor among training analysts.

Moreover, 55 percent of IAAP training analysts say active imagination is considered to be an optional component in training.

Of the respondents, 56 percent believe it is seen as a secondary method; however, in reality, 78.8 percent of IAAP members, routers, and trainees consider it a
fundamental component in training.

The percentage asking for more practical exercises on such content through experiential workshops is 83.7 percent. In addition, 42.2 percent of IAAP members,
routers, and trainees consider active imagination to be a fundamental component
in training, showing a further discrepancy between how individuals perceive active
imagination and how they believe it is considered in the IAAP Association they
are part of. Actually, 78.8 percent of IAAP members, routers, and trainees say that
active imagination is a fundamental component in training, but only 33 percent of
training analysts believe active imagination is considered to be an essential method
in the Association they are part of.

Data analysis validates the research hypothesis highlighting, among others, a
big discrepancy in the confidence shared by Jungian analysts who consider active

QUESTION: Is Active Imagination considered to be
an optional component in training?

Overall:

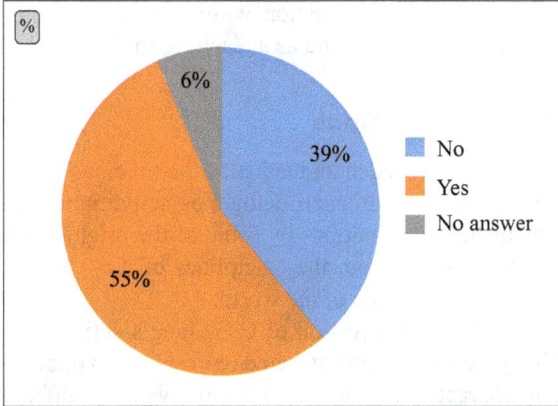

Figure 5 Percentage of IAAP training analyst respondents who believe and who do not believe active imagination is considered to be an optional component in training.

QUESTION: Do you consider Active Imagination
a fundamental component in IAAP training?

Overall:

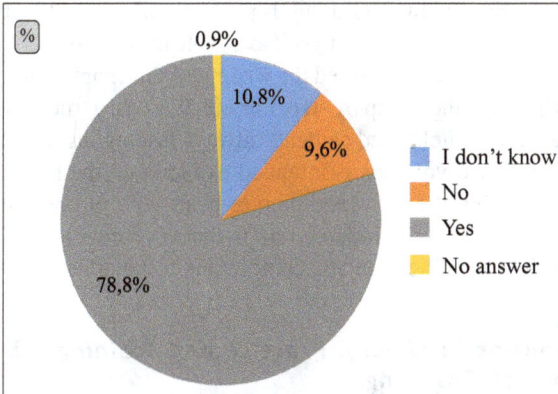

Figure 6 Percentage of IAAP member, router, and trainee respondents who believe, who do not believe, and who do not know if active imagination is considered to be a fundamental component in training.

imagination to be a fundamental practice both for C.G. Jung and for the Jungian community, and the current lack of knowledge, spread, use, and relevance of such practice by IAAP Jungian analysts and in IAAP training.

I believe all this material could represent some interesting food for thought on the relevance given to active imagination within the IAAP, both as theoretical knowledge and as clinical practice, and as a teaching subject in IAAP training.

Content and Aim of the Book

The aim of this book is to broaden and enhance the precious value of the special legacy of C.G. Jung, which he himself defined as active imagination, through a collection of unpublished contributions by some of the brightest Jungian analysts and renowned representatives from the disciplines of Art, Culture, Physics, and Neurosciences from different parts of the world.

About one century after the creation of C.G. Jung's active imagination, these voices put together give life to a multifaceted representation of active imagination, showing its many characteristics at a theoretical level, the different settings and ways in which such practice is currently used and experienced, and the resonance that active imagination can have in the scientific, artistic, and cultural fields.

The book not only targets the Jungian community, psychologists, and psycho-analysts in general, but also anyone in the world who may be interested in discovering the possible correlation between an original and fascinating psychotherapeutic practice such as active imagination, and the content in the fields of Neuroscience, Physics, Cinema, Literature, Painting, Music, and Dance.

I invited both fellow Jungian analysts and friends from the worlds of Art, Culture, Physics, and Neurosciences to work on this book, with the goal of offering the reader a kaleidoscopic representation of the extent to which active imagination, as conceived and experienced by C.G. Jung, is present. I allowed all authors complete freedom, and at the same time made myself available to collaborate, clarify, amplify, and listen. In fact, I can say I supported the writing of the chapters for at least half of the participants, helping them step by step. For me, this was a true way of diving into varied and differentiated fields and contents, always fascinating and interconnected.

The division into two volumes is intended to facilitate the reader's orientation in different subjects, but the areas and themes dealt with in both volumes are absolutely related to one another. Indeed, I hope that each chapter pushes readers to look for the possible amplification and completion in the others.

Active Imagination in Theory, Practice and Training. The Special Legacy of C.G. Jung

This volume mainly addresses the history, theory, clinical practice, and personal experimentation, as well as reflections on the teaching of active imagination. By simultaneously addressing the theoretical aspects and the practical application of active imagination through the method of "authentic movement", the last chapter is a sort of *trait d'union* between the first and the second volume.

Interdisciplinary Understandings of Active Imagination. The Special Legacy of C.G. Jung

In this volume, I deliberately wanted to give space to the close correlation between active imagination and the soma: the body, emotions, sensations, and feeling come into play, in the experience of active imagination, no less than what Jung defined as the "thinking function". Particular space is devoted, in this regard, to illustrating the practice of active imagination in the form of "authentic movement". This volume is also made up of the contributions and amplifications provided by the representatives from the worlds of Physics, Neurosciences, Cinema, Literature, Painting, Dance, and Music. This proves that all these areas can in some way have to do with active imagination.

Ways Participants Contributed to This Book

While, as already mentioned, fellow Jungian analysts had complete freedom of choice on the content to be developed, I asked the representatives of Art, Culture, Physics, and Neuroscience to compare their work with the four phases of active imagination, as described by M.L. von Franz (1980) as follows:

Phase 1: The first phase of active imagination can be defined as letting things happen. A deliberate emptying of one's mind, which Jung defined as doing-by-not-doing, a receptive abandonment, an inclination to opening up to images characterized by unselfconsciousness, and devoid of conscious controls, corrections, and denials.

Phase 2: The second phase of active imagination occurs when you can also accept the irrational and incomprehensible, because they both represent the process of becoming. An acceptance capable of allowing the unconscious images to surface to the consciousness.

Phase 3: The third phase of active imagination is that of recording of images transforming themselves. The progressive change of the contents of imagination is carefully followed and described, either by writing down the images or expressing them through other means, such as painting, sculpture, music, dance, etc.

Phase 4: In the fourth phase, when active imagination comes to life, an actual dialogue with the unconscious takes place, through an "ethical confrontation" with anything that was previously created. It is the individual stance, fundamental to really come to terms with one's inner images and Shadow. Jung turns the metaphor of theater around, speaking of "making the scene".

Last but not least, as rightly pointed out by Joan Chodorow, "later on" to these four phases, "she (von Franz, Ed.) adds: Apply it to ordinary life" (Chodorow, 1997, p. 11). This recommendation once again shows that active imagination cannot be compared to a technique since it suggests making active imagination natural and connatural to our way of being in the world. And this is directly related to what

I highlighted with regards to an attitude of active imagination and the consequent different way of being in the world.

I am extremely grateful to all analyst colleagues from the Jungian community for the stimulating contributions and analysis on active imagination provided to my research. I am also grateful to all my friends who are representatives of the worlds of Art, Culture, Physics, and Neurosciences for accepting the invitation to a confrontation with active imagination in relation to their professional field. It was extremely fascinating for me to receive their resonance, as a result of "only" perceiving the four phases of active imagination.

After two years of work, and thanks to the special legacy of active imagination passed on to us by C.G. Jung, interviewing and carrying out this research with the participants, through an ongoing dialogue and shared path, resulted in the creation of a very meaningful and fascinating interdisciplinary bridge.

I trust this fascination will reach all readers.

The Spark of Ethical Confrontation

As I said at the beginning of this chapter, this book on active imagination can be defined by two statements by C.G. Jung. The first, as previously described, is related to my initial and distant encounter, in 1978, with "the prime matter" at the core of Jung's work, namely active imagination. The second, on the other hand, had an affectively special function for me in the genesis of the research behind this book.

Between 2020 and 2021, during the difficult period of the COVID-19 pandemic, I decided to write a novel (Tozzi, 2022) on this: the search for something meaningful that has been lost, and which is essential to find again. Just as I was finishing reviewing the manuscript and reflecting on the title I had chosen, i.e. *La scintilla necessaria* (The Necessary Spark), I found myself rereading the last volume of Jung's *Letters III* (Jung, 1997), written between 1956 and 1961. And a sentence from one of them particularly struck me. The letter is dated 22 December 1958, and is addressed to Baroness Vera von der Heydt. Jung speaks precisely of active imagination, and how its application has been misinterpreted. Finally, he concludes: "From such discussion we see what awaits me once I have become posthumous. Then everything that was once fire and wind will be bottled in spirit and reduced to dead nostrums. Thus are the gods interred in gold and marble and ordinary mortals like me in paper" (Jung, 1975: 469).

As usual, the images Jung delivers are extremely powerful. And the image of Jung prefiguring himself buried only in paper resonates painfully. Even in later letters in 1960, Jung appears concerned about the fate of what he was attempting to convey which was not understood or was misunderstood.

Here, that reading, at such a collectively heavy and dark time, seemed to me an event related to synchronicity. I had just finished writing a story where it seems fundamental to keep "the necessary spark" alive: but what was I doing about the precious legacy handed down to us by Jung, to keep his spark alive? Such a question seemed to have a lot to do with that "ethical confrontation" which, for Jung, is the final goal of active imagination.

This is why that very evening I decided that, although the undertaking seemed disproportionate, I should try to start a research into active imagination.

First of all, I wrote to Murray Stein. Then, one by one, to other colleagues and friends.

And they all picked up that spark with me.

Notes

1 *Le parole sono altrove*, by Gruppo Cinema A.I.P.A, presented at the Congresso Nazionale A.I.P.A (Napoli 2000), and 15th IAAP International Congress, Cambridge, UK, August 2001.

2 *Un doppio fondo* [A double meaning] [Video], by Chiara Tozzi, Congresso Internazionale AIPA-IAAP "Jung 50 anni dopo", Roma, 2011.

3 Special thanks go to my colleague Tom Kelly. I don't think I would have had the courage to continue working on that research at the international level without his enthusiastic feedback after the viewing of *Doppio fondo* in Rome.

4 As part of the Fourth Joint Conference IAAP and IAJS: "Psyche, Spirit and Science: Negotiating Contemporary Social And Cultural Concerns", Yale University, New Haven, CT, July 2015.

5 *The Lighting of Shadow Images – Interview with Giuseppe Tornatore by Chiara Tozzi* was screened for the first time at the IAAP International Film and Analytical Psychology Conference, Belgrade, 2–4 June 2023.

6 I am extremely grateful to the IAAP officers back then: IAAP: Toshio Kawai (President), Misser Berg (President Elect), Pilar Amezaga (Vice President), Emilija Kihel (Vice President), Yasuhiro Tanaka (Honorary Secretary), as well as Pilar Amezaga and Grazina Gudaite, Co-Chair of the IAAP Academic Sub-Committee, for encouraging and supporting me in a task that, at the time, seemed just as big as it was risky. I am also grateful to the IAAP Secretary Selma Gubser for the patient and kind support provided with regards to sending and receiving back the questionnaire from all IAAP members.

7 Robert Mercurio translated the chapter by IAAP colleague Federico de Luca Comandini from Italian into English.

8 Regina Renn worked with me in developing the research. Although she decided from the start not to provide a written contribution, I am grateful for her ongoing support, advice, and encouragement.

9 Giorgio Banchieri, ASIQUAS National Secretary, DiSSE, Department of Social and Economic Sciences, teacher, Sapienza University of Rome and *Sapienza* e LUISS Business School, Rome; Paolo Fornelli, Researcher at DiSSE, Department of Social and Economic Sciences, Sapienza University of Rome, ASIQUAS member; Maria Piane, Researcher at the Faculty of Medicine, *Sant'Andrea*, Sapienza University of Rome, ASIQUAS member.

References

Adler, G. (1948) *Studies in Analytical Psychology*, London and New York: Routledge, 1999.

Atmanspacher, H., Primus, H., and Wertenschlag-Birkhauser, E. (eds.). (1995) *Der Jung-Pauli Dialog und seine Bedeutung fur diemoderne Wissenschaft* [The Jung–Pauli Dialogue and Its Significance for Modern Science], Berlin: Springer.

Chodorow, J. (ed.) (1997) *Jung on Active Imagination*, New York: Routledge.

Colangeli, V. (2022) "Active imagination": Interview with Dr. Chiara Tozzi", AIPA. https://www.youtube.com/watch?v=9WSrMg_wVuI

Garufi, B. (2002) "La Poesia" [Poetry], in *L'Immaginazione Attiva, a cura di De Luca Comandini e Robert Mercurio* [*The Active Imagination* edited by De Luca Comandini and Robert Mercurio]. Milan: La Biblioteca di Vivarium.

Garufi, B., and Pavese, C. (1959) *Fuoco grande*, Turin: Einaudi. [Pavese, C. (1963), *The Beach: And, A Great Fire*, in Collaboration with Bianca Garufi., London: P. Owen Publisher.]

Jung, C.G. (1916/58) "The Transcendent Function", *Collected Works*, Vol. 8, Princeton: Princeton University Press, 1975.

Jung, C.G. (1961) *C.G. Jung, Memories, Dreams, Reflections*, London: Fontana Press 1995.

Jung, C.G. (1975) "Letters, Volume 2: 1951–1961", G. Adler & A. Jaffè (eds), Princeton: Princeton University Press.

Jung, C.G (1996) *Lettere, III*, Magi Edizioni, Rome 2006, p. 185 (C.G. Jung, *Briefe*, Patmos VerlagGmbHo, KG, Walter-Verlag, Dusseldorf, 1997).

Jung, C.G. (2009) *The Red Book: Liber Novus*, New York: Norton.

Stein, M. (2017) "Synchronizing Time and Eternity: A Matter of Practice" in *Outside, Inside and All Around*, Asheville, North Carolina: Chiron Publications.

Tozzi, C. (2014) "En Route: From Active imagination to Film Language" in *Proceedings of the 19th Congress of the International Association for Analytical Psychology*, Daimon Verlag.

Tozzi, C. (2015) "Jung &Nabokov", in Succedeoggi.it https://www.succedeoggi.it/2015/12/jung-nabokov/

Tozzi, C. (2017) "A Different Way of Being in the World: The Attitude of the Patient Script-writer", *Journal of Analytical Psychology* 62(2), April 2017.

Tozzi, C. (2017) "A Different Way of Being in the World" in *Proceedings of the 20th Congress of the International Association for Analytical Psychology*, Daimon Verlag.

Tozzi, C. (2022) *La scintilla necessaria* [The Necessary Spark]. Mondadori, Milan.

Tozzi, C. (2023) "Active Imagination and Testament: A Window on the Other Side of Life", in *Individuation Psychology: Essays in Honor of Murray Stein*, Chiron.

Tozzi, C., *et al.* (2000) *Le parole sono altrove* [Words are elsewhere]. Film by Gruppo Cinema AIPA, Congresso Nazionale AIPA, Naples.

Tozzi, C., *et al.* (2001) *Le parole sono altrove* [Words are elsewhere]. Film produced by Gruppo Cinema AIPA, 15th IAAP International Congress IAAP, Cambridge, UK.

Von Franz, M.L. (1980) "On Active Imagination", in *Inward Journey: Art as Therapy*, 17 (La Salle and London: Open Court, 1983).

Von Franz, M.L. (1988) *Il mondo dei sogni*, Tea Due, p. 102, Milan, 1996 [*The Way of Dream*, by Fraser Boa, Windrose Films Ltd, Toronto, 1988].

Chapter 2

The Origin and History of Embodied Active Imagination

Authentic Movement through the Life and Work of Its Early Pioneers

Karin Fleischer

Introduction

This chapter offers an introduction to a developing somatic approach based on Active Imagination, known as Authentic Movement. It begins with an overview about its origins as well as later developments, through the work of the early contributors. It follows with an interview I did with Jungian analyst and international teacher, Dr. Tina Stromsted, which illustrates some theoretical and clinical elements key to this somatic-symbolic practice.

Initially described as an exploration of the unconscious psyche through somatic experience, this approach has evolved in the last few decades. Bringing in new elements from the neuroscientific field, it has expanded its clinical applications toward working with early relational trauma, psychosomatic disorders, and other clinical conditions we frequently find in our consulting rooms – for which an interpretative, solely verbal-explicit approach is insufficient.

Early Beginnings – Tina Keller-Jenny

As we know, C.G. Jung discovered Active Imagination between 1913–1916 following his tumultuous break with Sigmund Freud. In a state of disorientation and profound inner turmoil he found a natural way to heal himself from within. Engaging with the feelings, impulses, fantasies, and images that arose from his unconscious, he gave them form through writing, painting, and sculpting and then brought them to further consciousness through reflecting on what they could mean – a kind of "symbolic play" that became the foundation of his emerging analytical psychological method (Chodorow, 1997, pp. 1–2). Tina Keller-Jenny, a lover of dance with a deep interest in the inner world, underwent many years of analysis with C.G. Jung and Toni Wolff, during 1915–1928, and discovered movement as active imagination (Swan, 2009). Closing her eyes, she opened to the unconscious as it found expression through her body, bringing awareness to the bodily sensations, movement impulses, emotions, and images that arose during her analytic hours, witnessed by Toni Wolff. In the process, Keller-Jenny was able to resolve some of her most binding psychological complexes, becoming an early practitioner

DOI: 10.4324/9781003411383-2

in integrating body-based/movement approaches into analysis. Later she went on to train as a medical doctor, becoming a Jungian-oriented psychiatrist, and mother of five children. Having moved from Switzerland to Los Angeles, following the death of her husband in 1963, she worked with patients in a psychiatric hospital in Los Angeles, integrating movement approaches together with world-renowned Swiss dancer and mime, Trudi Schoop, who was one of the pioneers of the new field of Dance Movement Therapy.

The Origin of Authentic Movement – Mary Starks Whitehouse

During the 1950s, Mary Starks Whitehouse – another pioneer in the field of Dance Movement Therapy, as well as a modern dancer, with a rich background in professional dance training, teaching, and performing spanning a professional diploma from the Wigman Central Institute in Dresden, Germany, to the Martha Graham School in New York – engaged in personal analysis with Jungian analyst Hilde Kirsch. Kirsch had been analyzed by C.G. Jung in Zürich. Both Whitehouse and Kirsch had settled in Los Angeles after coming from Europe, and through Kirsch's influence, Whitehouse studied at the C.G. Jung Institute in Zürich. Although she did not graduate from that Institute, her personal analysis as well as her studies in analytical psychology influenced her development of a psychosomatic approach to unconscious personality (Frantz, 1972). She immersed herself, along with her students, in this exploration, aiming to find the inner source of expressive movement. Some of these early explorations were presented as lecture-demonstrations to members of the Analytical Psychology Club of Los Angeles and at UCLA (Whitehouse, 1958/1999; 1963/1999).

One of Whitehouse's greatest contributions has been her understanding of body movement as an expression of unconscious contents, elements she explored in depth with her students and clients as she witnessed their movement. Whitehouse established the difference between the experience of "being moved" ("I am moved") – as an expression of a somatic experience emerging from the unconscious psyche – from "I move" – as a manifestation of ego control and directness. In her words: "one has to learn 'to let it happen' as contrasted to doing it".[1]

> Ideally, both are present in the same instant, and it may be literally an instant. It is a moment of total awareness, the coming together of what I am doing and what is happening to me. It cannot be anticipated, explained, specifically worked for, nor repeated exactly . . . . Just as the body changes in the course of working with the psyche, so the psyche changes in the course of working with the body. We would do well to remember that the two are not separate entities but mysteriously a totality.[2]

This comprehension has opened the way to conceiving the body sensory somatic affective expression as an experience of active imagination without having to be linked to a particular form of movement or any other art form, thus enlarging Jung's perspective on Active Imagination.

In one of the lectures offered at the Analytical Psychology Club of Los Angeles at the beginning of the 1960s, she described Active Imagination in sensory terms:

> Following the inner sensation, allowing the impulse to take the form of physical action is active imagination in movement, just as following the visual image is active imagination in phantasy. It is here that the most dramatic psychophysical connections are made available to consciousness.[3]

When body experience follows the inner impulse, there is usually an element of surprise, it emerges unexpectedly, like "dreams – vivid, ephemeral, full of affect".[4]

Whitehouse initially called her work Movement-in-Depth, and later, Authentic Movement. In her paper "C.G. Jung and Dance Therapy. Two Major Principles", she writes: "Movement-in-depth, derived from my own experience of Jungian analysis, means 'Physical Movement as a revelation of the Self'".[5] She was working on a book about the development of her work, *The Moving Self*, but, sadly, could not finish it. Nevertheless, her pioneering contribution has grown and expanded in many parts of the world throughout the work of new generations of dance movement therapists and analysts who continue to value the body as a path towards the Self.

Active Imagination in Movement – Joan Chodorow

Several of Whitehouse's students – Janet Adler, Zoë Avstreih, Penny Bernstein, Joan Chodorow, Irma Dorsamantes-Alperson, Carolyn Grant Fay, Wendy Wyman – continued to build on the foundations of her work (Chodorow, 1991). Two of them, Joan Chodorow (1991, 1997, 1999) and Janet Adler (1995, 1996, 2002) became recognized international teachers, developing training programs in Authentic Movement in the United States and Europe, which have expanded the development of this approach within the fields of Dance Movement Therapy and Analytical Psychology.

Drawing from a background that encompasses early studies in Dance Movement Therapy and a doctorate degree in theology, Adler has further explored the role of the witness/analyst. The understanding of the analyst as witness, means that she/ he "does not interpret the emerging unconscious contents, but uses its own body-psyche-presence as a holding, mirroring and resonating surface for the patient's body's inner experience".[6] Another important contribution has been Adler's experiential and theoretical exploration of the collective and mystical dimensions of the work (Adler 1992, 1996). Moreover, she developed one of the first training programs in Authentic Movement, bringing a developmental perspective of the form into the experiential-learning process.

Chodorow, a Dance Movement therapist and Jungian analyst from the C.G. Jung Institute of San Francisco, has deepened the understanding of body movement as active imagination within the field of Analytical Psychology. Together with Wendy Wyman, Carolyn Grant Fay, Marion Woodman, Tina Stromsted, and other analyst colleagues, Chodorow has co-facilitated Sunday Pre-Congress workshops on Authentic Movement, Danced and Moving Active imagination at IAAP Congresses, every three years going back to IAAP Cambridge, England in 2001, a tradition that continues today. Since the focus of this research project is on Active Imagination, I will now focus on Chodorow's work, introducing the themes she has explored and written about (1991, 1997, 1999).

In her book *Dance Therapy and Depth Psychology: The Moving Imagination*, Chodorow writes: "When we used our bodies to express the imagination, the vividness of the sensory-motor experience tends to take us to complexes that were constellated in infancy or early childhood."[7] The seeds of this notion were already present in many of her early papers written between 1977 and 1986.

Chodorow's first attempt to delve deeper into the connection between Jung's active imagination and the practice of Authentic Movement was included in her paper "Dance Therapy and the Transcendent Function" (1978/1999). Six years later, "To Move and Be Moved" (1984) presented her exploration into the origins of the movement experience in the psyche. Chodorow expresses that the process of active imagination in movement can be extremely complex, but that with enough sensitivity and careful attention, one may begin "*to see patterns*".[8] She adds:

> Movement from the cultural unconscious is our bridge to mythic images, and the development of cultural forms. Movement from the primordial unconscious may, for brief moments, put us in touch with the completely untransformed primal affects. Movement from the ego-Self axis of identity gives us the experience of being moved by the ordering and centering process of the psyche.[9]

In "The Body as Symbol" (1986), she expands her exploration of specific somatic patterns while focusing on five symbolic themes that often manifest in movement and seem to reflect distinct stages of consciousness development in early childhood. In later papers and presentations at various conferences, Chodorow seeks to articulate her experiential and theoretical knowledge of *the moving imagination* with the primordial Affects researched by her co-researcher and late husband, Jungian analyst Louis H. Stewart (Chodorow, 2001).

Throughout her theoretical and clinical work, Chodorow has shown us how the "moving imagination" can take us to the emotional core of the complex, and can also lead us through it (Chodorow, 1991). Moreover, she has described the sensory-movement path of the archetypal imagination, showing how "in addition to direct experience of raw emotion, the imagination creates symbolic images and stories that express emotion in a way that may be more bearable".[10] In Authentic Movement these stories become embodied, enabling a development of a symbolic intra-intercorporeal container for the archetypal psyche.

Her contribution of body/movement as Active Imagination has been further developed by new generations of Jungian analysts who were able to integrate these insights with new elements, emerging from neuroscientific and early development contemporary research.

New Contributions: An Interview with Tina Stromsted

During the last two decades, awareness about the importance of considering the body in clinical treatment has grown due to new research concerning early developmental and complex trauma, affective neuroscience, and attachment theory. New dialogues have become possible. Thus, in 2005, Tina Stromsted organized a seminal conference at the C.G. Jung Institute of San Francisco, entitled "Soul's Body: Archetypal Defences, Affect Regulation, and Healing from Trauma", which brought together Joan Chodorow, Marion Woodman, Donald Kalsched, Stromsted herself, and pioneering neuroscience researcher, Allan Schore. Integrating theoretical presentations, panel discussions, and experiences in active imagination in movement, this event gave rise to a series of related conferences in the United States and Canada.

An increasing body of literature brought about new foundations for those analysts who, in working with Active Imagination from a sensorimotor perspective, have been developing ways to articulate that which happens before and beyond words when the body is included in the consulting room. Both imagination and the modes of intervention based on empathy have gradually gained more relevance as implicit modes of knowing, communication, and interventions versus the more traditional, explicit ways of working through interpretations (Fleischer, 2020).

At the same time, it has become clear how many of the elements that research has revealed in scientific terms were already present in the practice of these women, pioneers in working with the intra and inter-corporeality. The following interview, conducted 20 years ago, is an expression of this experiential knowledge, bringing forth meaningful, core elements related to the form of Authentic Movement, as well as Tina Stromsted's unique contribution, an integrative approach she calls "Soul's Body" (Stromsted, 2015). It also offers another piece of the historical development of this symbolic embodied approach within the field of Analytical Psychology.

All these women have shown in their work with an embodied form of Active Imagination how the learning process must also take place in the body. Integrative learning is not possible if the embodied experience is not included. And this, in turn, requires many years of delving into the unconscious, letting the body be the guide, in the presence of a witness/analyst who holds a safe container for this depth process to unfold.

From Body to Word: An Interview with Tina Stromsted,[11] PhD, BC-DMT[12]

I met Tina Stromsted more than ten years ago while I was completing a Master's program in dance/movement therapy and taking part in an Authentic Movement in-depth training group with Janet Adler. That happened between the end of the 1980s and beginning of the 1990s. I had heard Tina speak at several events and professional conferences and decided to begin a therapeutic process with her, integrating movement, creative arts, and Jungian Depth Psychotherapy. I recall the first day I walked into her studio on Cole Street in San Francisco to meet her. My body can still remember the permission I found to be myself. Tina's caring, patient work and focused attention helped me learn to differentiate between archetypal energies and more personal, developmental material. Discerning the interrelationship between the two became an essential part of our work. This was particularly important when the upwelling of archetypal energy emerging from my Authentic Movement explorations became too threatening.

Also known as "active imagination in movement", Authentic Movement is an embodied, therapeutic approach. In this practice, the patient/mover closes his/her eyes, allowing himself/herself to listen for and be moved by sensations, movement impulses, feelings, and images that emerge from deeper layers of the unconscious. As the patient/mover follows his/her experience, the analyst/ witness sits to the side of the space, with eyes open, attending to his/her own experience as he/she tracks the movement of the patient/ mover. Drawing or writing often follow the mover's experience. Then mover and witness speak together, without judgment or interpretation. This process helps the mover bring more consciousness to what is emerging than can often be reached in strictly verbal psychotherapy.

Ten years after completing my studies[13] and work with Tina, in 2001, I returned to the San Francisco Bay area to visit friends and teachers and to reconnect with my roots in Authentic Movement, having since become a teacher of this approach in my native Argentina. Sensing this as a turning point in my own life and work, I wanted to better understand the influences of my mentors, and interviewed Tina about the development of her work as a dance and somatic psychotherapist and international teacher of this work.

On a cool winter afternoon, in the same studio on Cole Street, Tina received me graciously, pouring tea as we began our conversation. Wanting to understand the roots of her practice – how her life experience had led her to this path – I asked her about her earliest beginnings with dance. "I don't ever remember a time without dance," she responded. "It was an important part of my childhood and adolescence. Expressing my feelings through movement gave me an enormous sense of freedom and wellbeing. Now I understand that it was soul-work, connecting me to what was most truthful in myself, and simultaneously to all of life."

Tina explained that she entered the scientific world of psychology through the body, as many dance/movement therapists have done. She studied with dance therapists Trudi Schoop, Norma Canner, Tamara Greenberg, and many others, while at the same time exploring the world of the body and psyche from other perspectives with Somatics pioneer Stanley Keleman, Reichian analyst Myron Sharaf, breath worker Magda Proskauer, Process-Oriented Jungian analyst Arnold Mindell, and mythologist Joseph Campbell. Later, through dance therapist and Jungian analyst, Joan Chodorow, she was introduced to Authentic Movement.

Feeling completely at home with this discipline, and recognizing the depth of what emerged, she pursued nine years of intensive training with dance therapist, Janet Adler. This brought back resonances of Tina's early days with dance, reconnecting her with important developmental material, as well as the mystical core of the practice. Subsequently, Tina co-founded the Authentic Movement Institute (1992) with Dance Movement Therapist, Neala Haze, in Berkeley, California, a comprehensive program for the study and practice of Authentic Movement (Stromsted and Haze, 2007). She also offered courses throughout the United States, Europe, and in many parts of the world while integrating it into her private psychotherapy practice in San Francisco. Since the late 1980s she has continued to deepen her experience and understanding of related work in developing embodied feminine consciousness with Jungian analyst, Marion Woodman, and her team of movement and vocal specialists, Mary Hamilton, and Ann Skinner, and is now core faculty of the Marion Woodman Foundation.

Through discovering her own voice and standpoint, Tina continued to find ways to bridge the worlds of mind, body, and spirit. As her work grew, she began to offer her unique contribution to the fields of Somatics, Depth Analytic Psychology, and dance and creative arts psychotherapies.

Sipping tea together, our conversation explored her early beginnings:

Karin *Where are your roots? What do you recognize as the source of your work?*

Tina   I think our work, if it is a genuine calling, is rooted at a soul level in our earliest beginnings. My childhood was spent in nature, in rural Massachusetts. Some years ago, I remember asking students in a supervision group in Rome, "Who was your first witness?" Many responded, "My mother was my first witness," which I think is true for many people. My own sense is that Nature was my first witness. It was there that I felt most whole, most inspired, most myself and most directly connected with something larger. Whenever I needed to touch a place that was true in me, I would go into Nature, swimming in the pond, dancing in tall grass in the fields across the street, or in the woods among the birches and oak trees. I remember a special tree . . . With my back against its sturdy trunk and a sense of my roots in the ground I would read, cry, write my dreams and feelings, create poetry, or simply connect with the silence . . . the potent presence of nature, within and around me. When things were difficult in my family, I sought solace and companionship outdoors, often accompanied by my Irish Setter, Golden Retriever, and/or my long-haired calico cat, with whom I could express myself without censorship.

I remembered the time when finding myself feeling "homeless", I still carried the responsibilities of the eldest child in a growing household. So, my earliest questions gave rise to my work, which I call "Re-inhabiting the Female Body". Or, more broadly, "Soul's Body", as I often work with men as well. This feels meaningful to me because my sense is that, given the biases of our patriarchal culture, the women I grew up with did not feel good about being a woman – about life in a female body.

One of the things I discovered some years ago in my dissertation research was that most women who are drawn to Authentic Movement are often working on their mother problem. Most of the practitioners are women, and the leading teachers are women. Though, fortunately, more men are now entering the field, I experience this approach as a way to develop the feminine, receptive, and relational element within both women and men. The practice engages our capacity for sensing, for listening deeply to the body's wisdom. It teaches us how to hold the tension between will and surrender, intention, and receptivity, moving and being moved. This involves softening one's defences and the ego's need to control, surrendering to a deeper source of guidance by what Jung called the Self.

Mary Starks Whitehouse, the grandmother of Authentic Movement, said, "Movement, to be experienced, has to be 'found' in the body, not put on like a dress or a coat. There is that in us which has moved from the very beginning. It is that which can liberate us."[14] On the deepest level it is about the development of embodied consciousness: bringing out the light in the cells; awakening spirit in matter. This is a departure from the old religious idea that matter is dense, dumb, and without consciousness. That God is distant from us, and that spirit must descend into the body through the head.

The practice of Authentic Movement encourages us to bring a new level of receptivity and openness to our experience – a quality of attention, and an enhanced awareness of what is occurring in us, as witness, and what we experience of the person who is moving. Over time, the process allows the light in the body to become aware of itself, and to develop. As movers and witnesses, we begin to feel more porous on a cellular level, more open, spacious, and better able to tolerate a deeper and wider range of emotions and energetic experiences, as we discover previously unknown or "shadow" parts of ourselves. The essence of the process is about being open to the unknown – embracing mystery. Over time, we become better able to live with ambiguity, developing a more compassionate, symbolic attitude, rather than seeking refuge in concrete ways of thinking, polarizing our perceptions into categories of black and white, right, or wrong. Life becomes more spontaneous, creative, and nuanced, more deeply personal, as individuals allow themselves to become authentic to their own nature – more genuinely who they are.

The amazing thing is that the more authentically ourselves we become, the more readily we can connect with something deeply universal. So, there is the paradox: the deeper we go into our personal material, the more we connect with the archetypal energies in the collective unconscious. Janet Adler describes this as the "collective body" (Adler, 1996) and Marion Woodman speaks of it as the "communal body" (Woodman, Lecture, January 29, 2003). This is an essential part of the process of becoming a more conscious, mature individual. You are then, paradoxically, freer to participate in a contributing way within the culture.

Karin   *How does this developing process occur in Authentic Movement?*

Tina   Moving safely with a non-judgmental personal witness can invite a regression to early, often pre-verbal material. This is one of the benefits that Authentic Movement can offer, which is often beyond the scope of verbal psychotherapy. We cannot talk about the things that we experienced before we had language, but our body remembers. When the mover feels safe, the intimacy of the mother–infant dyad often re-emerges; unresolved issues tend to surface, and the mover again experiences a longing to be seen as she is by her witness.

If we practice in the context of a psychotherapeutic relationship, we have the chance to revisit, explore, and support the slow, careful work of exploring the memories, dreams, feelings, and fantasies that emerge. These experiences can also emerge in the context of a group, resulting in inevitable transferences onto the group leader and to other group members, but there often is not the same opportunity to work it through. In the "collective body" work there tends to be more emphasis on sibling relationships, a sense of "belonging", of membership within the group. Inevitably, however, there is often parental or spiritual transference onto the group leader, but with less emphasis on each individual's personal history. Rather, the focus is often on the stories and themes that group members discover and co-create together. Sourced in the depths of the body–psyche connection, these stories often mirror myths and fairy tales from many cultures and periods in history, reflecting human dilemmas, roles, and collective energies that seek form anew in each generation.

Karin   *What do you think about the potential of Authentic Movement when is included in the psychotherapeutic process?*

Tina   It is potentially transformative. We need to know how to hold a safe container and be present for the mover when unconscious material emerges. Impressions, beliefs, feelings, self-definitions – so much is stored in the cells and finds form through the person's movement. Then the mover has an opportunity to explore and find words for what is being expressed in the movement. Otherwise, her feelings, images, memories, and associations can recede back into her body, where they continue to create disturbance, hold back her development, or even become further concretized through body symptoms and illness, as the system loses balance. A wide range of complexities naturally emerge when the body/psyche begins to open and the practice deepens, and these seek expression and further development within the dynamics of the relationship.

Karin   *What do you see coming into your own work from the experiences and training you have had with Trudi Schoop, Joan Chodorow, Janet Adler, and Marion Woodman?*

Tina   I was able to surrender some of my rational, protective, "independent" stance with Tamara Greenberg, who was my first therapist. Our work together helped me trust my kinesthetics experience, my somatic "ground", not only in nature but also in relationship to myself and to others. Trudi Schoop brought more access to a wide range of affects and imaginal experiences. She was an inspiring teacher and encouraged us to fully engage our feelings through expressive movement. She also helped me discover the "dreams" that my psyche was trying to express, moment by moment, through ordinary movements, such as walking, sitting, and for forth, and to embody these more fully in my life. Trudi was a professional mime and dancer in her early years and used her art to illuminate political issues and social injustice, which has always been important to me, as well.

Then I experienced Authentic Movement for the first time in a course with Joan Chodorow and continued to deepen my practice through many years of in-depth training with Janet Adler, eventually becoming her assistant and colleague. Trusting a woman to be able to see me, without judgment, criticism, envy, or blame – without projecting her feelings onto me, to the best of her ability – was really a new experience. Both women were able to do this. Though quite different in their styles, each was able to hold presence in ways that allowed me to explore my own experience at greater depth. As a Jungian analyst, dance therapist, and theorist, Joan has expanded my understanding of the psychological dimensions of active imagination in movement – the interpenetration of body and psyche. Together with her late husband, Jungian analyst Louis Stewart, she has made pioneering contributions to the study of affects, and the body's role in the healing process. Joan has a global perspective and is committed to working cross-culturally, which is an essential part of my work, as well.

Janet supported my investigation of direct, embodied experience. Her profound interest in the pre-symbolic dimensions of the mover's experience as well as the energetic, spirited phenomena that often develop over time in the practice mirrored my own early questions. These long-term, evolving relationships provided a foundation that I could trust, and now draw from, internally, in my work with others. Incidentally, both are mothers as well as professional women. Their individual experiences, questions, and authenticity have been deeply integrated in the work, another invaluable aspect of what they have modeled for me.

My studies with Marion Woodman have helped me continue to bridge Jung's analytic work with bodily experience, artistic process, and vocal expression. In the process, I have found more of my own voice and standpoint in the world. Marion's work with dreams is profound. Like Jung, her life is guided by them. In addition, her honesty in modeling a path of healing from an early eating disorder and a gripping addiction to perfection has helped me better understand the ways that our culture ravages the feminine. Her love of the sacred feminine and her commitment to supporting its embodiment in our world continue to inspire me, personally and professionally.

Dance therapists like Trudi, Tamara, Joan, and my first supervisor, Judi Bell, taught me about using structured, directive movement therapy interventions. Later I understood that this is what I had been exploring in my own way, both in my dance classes and with the patients in the hospital groups I facilitated. However, after studying different dance forms and practicing zazen sitting mediation, I felt most drawn to the self-directed experience of Authentic Movement. There, I did not have to follow outer direction, nor perform, but could touch something fresher, more unknown, and genuine within myself. This felt radical to me; it was a pathway to the Self, the deeply embodied feminine soul that had survived patriarchal programming and was longing to emerge. Authentic Movement provided a way to contact something more vulnerable – parts of myself that lay beneath all my conditioning – forgotten, unfamiliar, or underdeveloped. It also became my spiritual practice.

Years later, I developed a course to support women in embodying this material, while participating with other faculty in designing the curriculum for the newly forming Women's Spirituality Program at the California Institute of Integral Studies in San Francisco. In working experientially with the students, it was remarkable to see how, when they started exploring their inner experience through their bodies, they felt directly connected to a sacred source that was deeply feminine. They were amazed to discover images of the Goddess emerging from their bodies, through movement, art, and song. Some of them found specific goddess images in particular energy centers or chakras. Though they had seen images of these goddesses in books, it had not occurred to them that these energies were their birth right, resonant in their flesh, if they could only drop into their experience enough to listen . . .

Karin   *This is a source that lies beyond all conditioning, which cannot be contacted by will alone.*

Tina   Yes, and to reconnect with it we must risk opening to, and softening, the many layers of accommodation and defence that we have organized, psychologically and somatically. Along the way, there are often periods of profound grief, rage, fragmentation, dissolution, reorientation, new form, and renewed hope . . . because if I am not only that which I learned was "woman", then who am I? One can also see these phases in the ancient practices of alchemy and Shamanism – they are universal stages in the transformative journey, though they are experienced by each individual in unique ways. In the process, we must feel contained enough, supported enough, and loved enough to let the outer layers begin to melt to ask that question. That is how healing and growth occur. It is a very rigorous and humbling process, and I continue to learn a great deal from witnessing other women who are strong enough and flexible enough to go through it themselves. I also have enormous gratitude for my teachers, colleagues, and friends who have lent their guidance, support, and presence at various times along my path. This way of learning is a natural part of feminine development, as well. It is about relationship.

Karin   *How was it to bring your voice from the body into the patriarchal academic world through your dissertation?*

Tina   Particularly challenging! But in the end, it was a transformative experience. From time to time, over the last 20 years, I had investigated several PhD programs but never found one that would allow me to pursue my own interests. In the end, it was good that I waited to apply, because by then the educational system had begun to open a little more to include the body, the feminine, and the arts. This would not have been possible 20 years ago. This shift in the zeitgeist of the culture allowed me to include experiences from my movement practice and feedback provided by my dreams within the research process itself. My body became a profound source of learning, included in every aspect of the study. I also tracked my dreams and did drawings, both of my dreams and my movement experiences. Though it was a lot of work – a long, challenging process that involved a lot of reflective thinking – it was passionate, too! The two strands – the analytic and the creative – continually wove together, in a way that worked on me, from the inside out.

Because the process took place in an academic setting, it was a delicate situation. I was continually challenged to remain connected to my truth, while standing up to outer authorities to defend the value of my organic, integrative approach. Although it was difficult at times, I was able to substantiate the integrity of my research and process, without falling victim to the power complex – the well-known tendency to be the "dutiful daughter" who seeks approval from the "father" or outside authority figure – which is the *sine qua non* of the hierarchically based academic system. I not only had to confront a very painful impasse with a male professor, but I had to take responsibility for my own internalized patriarchy: the inner voices that tried to direct my work or tell me that it was never enough, nor good enough. At times I felt doubtful or lost because what I was doing felt so new. The methodology that I chose was very much like Authentic Movement; it was not about trying to prove a hypothesis conceived ahead of time, it was about discovering something as I went along. All of this was new at the time; I did not know anyone that had done it quite like that before, so I had to have enough trust, and keep going back to my body and to my dreams as primary sources. In recent years, increasing numbers of researchers are choosing qualitative methods, and it is heart-warming to see all the other women who are now including the experiences of body and psyche in their research.

Karin   *The experience of being recognized as who we are, including our feelings, has not been common throughout Western modern history. Could you say something about this sense of knowing, or embodied knowing? A knowledge that is not separate from the body, but "comes in and through" the body, as in the transformative process you just spoke about?*

Tina   Though there has been a lot of writing about the verbal psychotherapeutic process, and increasingly more about the role of the body in psychotherapy, what we have the chance to do in this kind of research is to deeply experience, reflect on, and articulate how transformation is a cellular process. It is not just something we think about or read about, but something we experience and live. For example, Marion Woodman was one of the women involved in the study. As I mentioned earlier, she is a Jungian analyst and author who works a great deal with the embodied sacred feminine. During one of our interviews, Marion described a woman analysand with whom she was working who was crying and suffering deeply. Marion spontaneously reached out to take her client's hand, feeling compassion and love for her, but the woman pulled away. It was a huge moment for both because the analysand realized that, though she thought she was feeling better about herself, she discovered that the hatred of the feminine was lodged in her cells, and that it went back to her mother, her grandmother, and her great-grandmother . . . all the way back through her feminine lineage. Marion then realized that it was not enough just to talk together but that her client's body needed to have the experience of feeling seen and "held" by a conscious, loving witness.

Karin *That is very moving. . . . I would also like go back to what you said earlier concerning the research process. You said that the process was not so much about having to prove something but one of discovery. What have you discovered?*

Tina I learned a good deal about the body's role in healing and change for women practicing Authentic Movement. This is true for men as well, though my research focused on women's experience. This included essential elements in the practice, and stages that often occur in what can be a profoundly transformative process. To do this, I interviewed a number of advanced practitioners in Authentic Movement; each came from a quite different background and theoretical framework. In the beginning, I invited each woman to speak broadly and openly about her experience, both personally and as a teacher and/or clinician in this work. During follow-up interviews, I asked them more specific questions. Over time, themes began to emerge repeatedly, which I then synthesized into major categories.

During the process, I developed an even deeper respect for the importance of creating a safe, conscious container. What constitutes a "conscious container?" We can use that word easily, but how you co-create or prepare a container involves a very subtle combination of elements that need to be made conscious. Most importantly, it requires the presence of an experienced witness or group of witnesses who can observe and bring a quality of presence to the work, without judgment or interpretation. This "safe enough" container is essential for enabling the mover to surrender to the unknown. It is what allows her the courage to soften her defences, to give up her socially conditioned "persona" identity, in order to descend into unconscious material.

Like Inanna or Persephone – two important early feminine figures from the ancient myths – the mover can descend to the "underworld", learn to integrate shadow material, and emerge as a more mature, individuated person. She moves from the psychological position of a "maiden" or girl to a "woman", through a profound process of descent and return.

My research questions had to do with discerning the conditions that were necessary to allow a woman to make this descent, to discover forgotten, rejected, or pre-conscious parts of herself, and then bring them to consciousness. It is like descending into a cave, discovering the treasure there, and bringing it back into daily life. This is a deeply embodied, transformative experience, echoing universal myths and initiation rites of passage, across cultures. I discovered that ancient initiation mysteries are still very much alive in us as modern people.

Karin   *Returning to how we began our conversation, I think about how our planet is now suffering and in grave danger too. Perhaps connecting to, and beginning the process of healing the Earth also needs to be through our relationship to our bodies?*

Tina   Exactly. I think the way we treat our planet is a direct reflection of the way we treat our bodies – a macrocosm of the microcosm. If we can trash our bodies with junk food, profound self-criticism, addictions, liposuction, plastic surgery, dramatic diets, lack of movement, time-pressures, abuse, and/or other disembodied ways of living, starving them or denying them in myriad ways, then we can trash the planet. We plunder her natural resources, without giving back. Actions led by this kind of unconscious or malignant attitude rape the planet, and we end up living at Her expense. This power-orientation, insensitivity, and need to control have profound costs: we forget how to listen to our deeper nature and to live in relationship to other cultures and to other species. To the extent that we are willing and able to listen to our own body-nature, we can also begin to resonate with the joy and suffering of others, and with the cycles of the earth. Embodied awareness is essential now. Trauma and fear work against this, breeding disassociation, numbness, and isolation – a profound disconnection from self and other. Trauma also collapses our ability to imagine the future and to invest in a better world. These are challenging times in our world, as corporate interests and fundamentalist religious beliefs are steering the policies and actions taken by our national government. This, in turn, has an enormous impact on the global human community and on the natural environment.

Authentic Movement and other forms of depth-oriented, embodied healing work provide a way home. The practice can reconnect us with ourselves, with each other, and with all of life. Numbness thaws and connection is re-established in a dance of creation that can renew us. Sometimes I invite students to move outdoors, where they experience themselves more fully in contact with Nature. They then may choose a small object to bring back into the studio and place it by their cushion/witness place before entering the circle as a mover. This is one of many small ways that we can bring consciousness to the presence of nature as our larger, "meta" witness. Then, in addition to the human witness who is sitting there, the mover can experience how she/he is held by concentric circles – spirals of connection and life.

Karin   *Since we are talking about images, what image comes to you as you reflect on the relationship between you and this work?*

Tina   There are many images, but two come most often. One is the Tibetan bowl. For many years, while sitting as a witness, I have had the sense of my pelvis as a singing bowl that resonates with deep, embodied knowing. The pelvis is the al-chemical hearth, the place in the body where we receive and hold our mover. It also cradles all our soft organs – the vitality of our lives. If we can be deeply grounded in our pelvis, in our own feminine nature, the mover can feel that much more held. Instead of being anxious, breathing high up in the chest, the witness is connected to the earth and to her own deep nature. The mover can then feel received, in a safe and embodied way.

The second image is of the lotus, a beautiful flower that unfolds over time, whose long root is planted deep in the mud beneath the water in which it floats. What begins in the mud, in that undifferentiated (and often undervalued) "prima materia"/elemental material, grows up into something magnificent and sacred. The two dimensions remain deeply connected throughout the process of growth and development. This natural image touches me deeply, reminding me of the organic wisdom inherent in the process, especially in moments when the work becomes challenging, cloudy, or painful.

Karin   *Thank you, Tina! Both symbols make me think about the capacity for rec-ognizing the light, by going in and through the darkness, and how important it is to have an embodied container for such a process to happen. It also brings the potential for new and more balanced relationships – with oneself, with one another, and with the Earth . . .*

Tina   Yes! Yes!

In Closing

The present overview has aimed to show how the inclusion of the body and the somatic dimension in the analytic practice, which can be traced back to the years of Tina Keller's working with C.G. Jung and Toni Wolff, has evolved into a sensory-motor form of Active Imagination, called Authentic Movement by early pioneer Mary Whitehouse. Since then, Authentic Movement has continued to gain in complexity, richness, and depth through the work of other generations of analysts who developed new foundations for the understanding of the process while remaining, at the same time, close to its core elements. In writing this piece of the history of Moving/Embodied Active Imagination, I wanted to show my gratefulness to these women who, by including the somatic-affective dimension of the Self in our clinical practice, have begun to heal a long inherited-wounded split between body–soul/psyche. They have taught many of us that there is no deep psychological transformation if the body is not included. As Marion Wood-man writes:

The one-sidedness of extreme spiritualization has produced only a "blear-eyed wisdom" born of "midnight oil". The tree of life does not unfold towards the fruit of individuation in this manner. Consciousness must share in the organic nature of the tree itself. The "brightening glance" of the Eight Eye of the eye of the healing serpent whose feminine power Christianity has largely ignored, must be allowed to penetrate in its darkest depths. Only then can the "great-rooted blossomer" stretch to its true height, sway to its true music, dance to the One dance.[15]

Notes

1 Whitehouse, M. (1963/1999, p. 53)
2 Whitehouse, M. (1963 / 1999 pp. 42–43).
3 Whitehouse, M. (1963/1999, p. 52).
4 Whitehouse, M. (1963/1999, p. 54).
5 Whitehouse, M. (1979/1999, p. 94).
6 Fleischer, K. (2020, p. 567)
7 Chodorow, J. (1991, p. 6).
8 Chodorow, J. (1991, p. 4; emphasis in original).
9 Chodorow, J. (1991, p. 4).
10 Chodorow, J. (2001, p. 9).
11 Tina Stromsted, PhD, MFT, LPCC, BC-DMT, RSME/T, is a Jungian Analyst, Board Certified Dance/Movement therapist, Somatic psychotherapist, author, and educator. Past co-founder and faculty of the Authentic Movement Institute in Berkeley, California. Faculty at the C.G. Jung Institute of San Francisco, Jung Platform, and the Marion Woodman Foundation. Founding faculty member of the Women's Spirituality Program at the California Institute of Integral Studies (CIIS) and core faculty member of the Somatics Psychology program (CIIS). She has taught for the Depth Psychology/Somatics Doctoral programs at Pacifica Graduate Institute, Santa Barbara Graduate Institute, the Institute of Transpersonal Psychology, numerous Jung Societies, Esalen Institute, Zist, and universities and healing centers internationally. Founder and director of Soul's Body Center®, she teaches and supervises Authentic Movement practitioners and teachers, psychotherapists, Creative arts therapists, and Somatic Psychotherapists in many parts of the world, supporting the development of embodied consciousness. She is a long-time co-facilitator of the Active Imagination in movement Pre-Congress Day for the International Association for Analytical Psychology with Joan Chodorow and analyst colleagues. With 45 years of clinical experience including hospitals, community mental health clinics, and private practice, her numerous articles, book chapters, and online webinars explore the integration of body, psyche, soul, culture, community, and nature in healing and transformation. With a background in dance and theatre, her work engages social activism, eco-psychology, reclaiming body wisdom, and living a life of soul as global citizens. Her private psychotherapy practice is in San Francisco, with international virtual consultation.
12 The interview took place in February 2001. The original version is longer. Sections have been chosen and edited to further illustrate the development of Authentic Movement for the present research project.
13 While completing a Master of Science in Dance Movement Therapy at California State University, East Bay, I was introduced to Authentic Movement by Neala Haze. Later, between 1987 and 1993, I did in-depth training in Authentic Movement with Janet Adler, and studied with Joan Chodorow the theoretical and clinical aspects of it from a Jungian perspective. Authentic Movement was also part of my analytic process with Tina Stromsted.
14 Whitehouse, M. (1963/1999, p. 53).
15 Woodman, M. (1980, p. 123).

References

Adler, J. (1992) Body and Soul. *American Journal of Dance Therapy*, 14, 2. Reprinted in P. Pallaro (Ed.), *Authentic Movement: Essays by Mary Starks Whitehouse, Janet Adler, and Joan Chodorow* (pp. 160–189). Philadelphia: Jessica Kingsley Publishers, 1999

Adler, J. (1995) *Arching Backward*. Vermont: Inner Traditions.

Adler, J. (1996) The Collective Body. *American Journal of Dance Therapy*, 18, 2. Reprinted in P. Pallaro (Ed.), *Authentic Movement: Essays by Mary Starks Whitehouse, Janet Adler, and Joan Chodorow* (pp. 190–204). Philadelphia: Jessica Kingsley Publishers, 1999.

Adler, J. (2002) *Offering from the Conscious Body*. Vermont: Inner Traditions.

Authentic Movement Institute (1992–2004). https://www.authenticmovementinstitute.com/

Chodorow, J (1978/1999). Dance Therapy and The Transcendent Function. *American Journal of Dance Therapy*, Spring/Summer. Reprinted in P. Pallaro (Ed.), *Authentic Movement: Essays by Mary Starks Whitehouse, Janet Adler, and Joan Chodorow* (pp. 236–252). London: Jessica Kingsley.

Chodorow, J. (1984). To Move and Be Moved. *Quadrant*, 17, 2, Fall. Reprinted in P. Pallaro (Ed.), *Authentic Movement: Essays by Mary Starks Whitehouse, Janet Adler, and Joan Chodorow* (pp. 267–278). London: Jessica Kingsley.

Chodorow, J. (1986). The Body as Symbol. Dance/Movement in Analysis. *The Body in Analysis, The Chiron Clinical Series*. Reprinted in P. Pallaro (Ed.), *Authentic Movement: Essays by Mary Starks Whitehouse, Janet Adler, and Joan Chodorow* (pp. 279–300). London: Jessica Kingsley.

Chodorow, J. (1991). *Dance Therapy and Depth Psychology: The Moving Imagination*. London: Routledge.

Chodorow, J. (1997). *Jung on Active Imagination*. Princeton, NJ: Princeton University Press.

Chodorow, J. (2001). *Emotions and The Archetypal Imagination*. Presented at the National Conference of Jungian Analysts, February 1–4, 2001.

Fleischer, K. (2020). The Symbol in the Body: The Un-doing of a Dissociation through Embodied Active Imagination in Jungian Analysis. *Journal of Analytical Psychology*, 65, 3, 558–583.

Frantz, G. (1972). An Approach to the Center. An Interview with Mary Whitehouse. *Psychological Perspectives*, 3, I, Spring. Reprinted in P. Pallaro (Ed.), *Authentic Movement: Essays by Mary Starks Whitehouse, Janet Adler, and Joan Chodorow* (pp. 17–28). Philadelphia: Jessica Kingsley Publishers, 1999.

Jung, C.G. (1930–34). *The Visions Seminars. Book One and Two*. Zurich: Spring Publications, 1976.

Stromsted, T. (2015). Authentic Movement & The Evolution of Soul's Body® Work. *Journal of Dance and Somatic Practices: Authentic Movement: Defining the Field, Intellect*, 7, 2.

Stromsted, T. and Haze, N. (2007). The Road In: Elements of the Study and Practice of Authentic Movement. In P. Pallaro (Ed.), *Authentic Movement: Moving the Body, Moving the Self, Being Moved: A Collection of Essays. Volume II* (pp. 56–68). Philadelphia: Jessica Kingsley Publishers, 1999.

Swan, W. (2009). *Memoir of Tina Keller-Jenny: A Lifelong Confrontation with the Psychology of C.G. Jung*. Spring Journal.

Whitehouse, M. (1958). The Tao of the Body. Paper presented at the Analytical Psychology Club of Los Angeles. Reprinted in P. Pallaro (Ed.), *Authentic Movement: Essays by Mary*

Starks Whitehouse, Janet Adler, and Joan Chodorow (pp. 41–50). Philadelphia: Jessica Kingsley Publishers, 1999.

Whitehouse, M. (1963). Physical Movement and Personality. Paper presented at the Analytical Psychology Club of Los Angeles. Reprinted in P. Pallaro (Ed.), *Authentic Movement: Essays by Mary Starks Whitehouse, Janet Adler, and Joan Chodorow* (pp. 51–57). Philadelphia: Jessica Kingsley Publishers, 1999.

Whitehouse, M. (1979). C.G. Jung and Dance Therapy. Two Major Principles. Reprinted in P. Pallaro (Ed.), *Authentic Movement: Essays by Mary Starks Whitehouse, Janet Adler, and Joan Chodorow*. Philadelphia: Jessica Kingsley Publishers, 1999.

Woodman, M. (1980). *The Owl Was a Baker's Daughter: Obesity, Anorexia Nervosa and the Repressed Feminine*. Toronto, Inner City Books.

Woodman, M. (January 29, 2003). Lecture in the Leadership Training Program, London, Ontario, Canada.

Chapter 3

Active Imagination
"When the Vague Images of the Psyche Can Be Touched with the Finger"

Ana Deligiannis

In the Beginning

Jung discovered Active Imagination during a critical period of his life (1913/1920), when he undertook the search for his own myth, getting in touch with the contents of his unconscious. In this period of disorientation and confusion, he needed to find a way to heal himself from within. Thus, engaged in such a Herculean task of facing his inner contents, he began to experience an attitude and at the same time a method, a way of knowledge, to explore the unknown. A work that started from an inner need ended up being a psychotherapeutic approach. Although it had different names, it was only in 1935, at a conference in Tavistock (London), that Jung gave it the name Active Imagination.

If we were to go back to the dawn of humanity, we would discover that man used imagination, in a broad sense, as a means to know God, gods, or the unknown. Therefore, in addition to being a method, it is a natural function of human psyche. This imaginative function of the psyche is one of the foundational concepts of Analytical Psychology.

Although there are many ways of accessing the unconscious (projective tests, dream interpretation, transferential interpretation), Active Imagination allows a direct encounter, a face-to-face confrontation with the reality of the unconscious.

In the journey Jung undertook, he wrote:

> After my separation from Freud, a period of inner insecurity, even disorientation, began for me. I felt that I was in the air, for I had not yet found my own place. I was mainly interested in finding a new attitude towards my patients.
>
> (Jung, 1981, p. 178)[1]

Since he did not know what to do, Jung decided to give himself consciously to the impulses and images of the unconscious. First, memories of his childhood (from the age of 10–11) arose, when he passionately played with stones and made constructions. In order to go back to that period and re-establish contact with it, he did so through his childhood games, despite his resistance and a certain *"painful feeling of humiliation, of not being able to do anything but play"* (ibid., p. 181).

DOI: 10.4324/9781003411383-3

This is how he rediscovered the symbolic play of childhood and began to unleash a number of fantasies that he then carefully wrote down.

At the same time, towards the end of 1913, he began to have catastrophic visions and dreams that were premonitory of the First World War. In order to find out what was happening to him and to find a meaning, he tried to translate his *"emotions into images, that is, to find those images that were hidden behind the emotions"* (ibid., p. 185). This was a turning point in his destiny, when he finally accepted the decision to play, to give himself over to the imagination, and get in touch with his fantasies.

This solitary journey that Jung undertook, in order to establish dialogues with the images of his unconscious, was first expressed in the *Black Book* (*Schwarze Buch*) and then in the *Red Book* (*Das Rote Buch or Liber Novus*) through calligraphic writings and colour paintings. It was an emotional and aesthetic experience that laid the foundation for the development of many theoretical concepts such as: active imagination, individuation process, shadow, *anima/animus*.

The "Imaginative Essence of the Soul". Image, Fantasy and Imagination

Jung states that "we live immediately only in the world of images" (1926, para. 624)[2] since "the psyche consists essentially of images" (ibid., para. 618) given that "all psychic activities create an image" (ibid, para. 616) and the "imaginative essence of the soul" takes a predominant place in psychic activity. According to him:

> The psyche creates reality daily. The only expression I can use for this activity is fantasy.[3] Fantasy is just as much feeling as thinking; as much intuition as sensation . . . . Fantasy seems to me the clearest expression of the specific activity of the psyche. It is, pre-eminently, the creative activity. . . . Fantasy has always been – and still is – the one who tends the bridge between the irreconcilable claims of the subject and object.
>
> (Jung, [1921] 1972, pp. 74–75)[4]

Imagination allows us to get in touch with the soul, constitutes an authentic psychic process (von Franz, 1982) and acts as a structuring nucleus of the psyche. Along the same line of thought, the philosopher Gaston Bachelard, as phenomenologist of creative imagination, states: "more than the will, more than the vital impulse, imagination is the very force of psychic production. Psychically, we are created by our fantasy . . . that delineates the furthest confines of our spirit" (in Geltman, 1996, p. 88).[5] Furthermore, he considers that imagination is the precursor of scientific discoveries. Every authentic invention is an exercise of Creative Imagination.

If we approach the alchemical *opus*, we may realize that the concept of imagination (*imaginatio*) also acquires a relevant meaning. In order to get in touch with the matter during the alchemist process, alchemists appealed to meditation, dreams, fantasies and imagination. As cited by Jung, Ruland says: "'Imagination is the *astrum* in man, the celestial or supercelestial body'. *Astrum* is the word that Paracelsus used and its meaning is approximately quintessence. . . *imaginatio* is thus a concentrated extract of life forces both physical and psychic" (Jung, 1957, pp. 298–299).[6]

From another perspective, Henry Corbin acknowledged in imagination a *productive* function, a real organ of knowledge, capable of "creating being", and not only a strictly *reproductive* function, a function to which it has been confined by Occidental philosophy from Plato onwards (Hillman, 1999). That is, it gives back to imagination its legitimate noetic value. Corbin speaks about creative imagination.

For Greek philosophers – Plato and Aristotle –, as well as in Middle Age, the image is considered as a representation, as a reproduction. With the hermetic philosophy and the alchemy, on the one hand, and with Kant, on the other, it is not only proposed a productive function of images (besides the reproductive one) but the creation of images is an indispensable condition to knowledge (Kugler, 1999).

Our psyche is composed of images; our being is an *imaginal*[7] being (Hillman, 1999) and as the psychic world is an *imaginal* world, the path of the imagination is the *via regia*, the real path to become in touch with the soul. A bridge between the consciousness and the unconscious, between the subject and the object, between the ideas and the things (Kugler, 1999), between the internal and the external world. For Chodorow (1994), the nature of imagination, besides being a symbolic process, leads us to the emotional core of complexes.

Active Imagination as a Method

While Active Imagination is an attitude that constitutes a foundational aspect of Analytical Psychology, it is also a method, a way of knowledge. Active Imagination is a process of dialogue that allows the exploration of the unconscious and enhances the communication between conscious and the contents of the unconscious. It is like a bridge that joins both riversides.

Beginning with one's own fantasies, dreams, emotional states or bodily sensations – as a starting point – these express themselves through images (which may be visual, tactile, auditory, olfactory, cenesthesic, kinesthesic) and allow us to be in touch with complexes and archetypes.

Marie-Louise von Franz (Dallet, 1982, Chodorow, 1997) proposes four stages in the process of Active Imagination for better comprehension and study:

First, the mind should be emptied; the "mad mind" should be stopped (meditation techniques cooperate in this stage). Ego thoughts should be set aside, the critical attitude should be suspended, in order to reach a state similar to the *alfa* state.

Second, let the images of the unconscious emerge, to make themselves present. In his comments on *The Secret of the Golden Flower* of 1929, Jung refers to this stage in terms of "wu-wei" of the Taoists, "not to interfere in the natural course of things" (Chodorow, 1997): to let things happen (*geschehenlassen*), welcome them and concentrate on the emerging material (*betrachten*); to look at the images without a critical attitude, to be interested in them, to "stick" to them so that they speak for themselves, and to pay attention to their development. They can appear in the form of images, impulses, emotions, sensations or movements; thus, the invisible becomes visible to us. Dialogues can also be established with the images.

The third stage is the moment of shaping them in an external expression through: words (oral description of the images), writing (stories, tales, poetry), drawing, painting, sculpture, movement, drama, collage. Active Imagination is a unique method, but it can be expressed in different ways.

Fourth is the ethic confrontation with what has emerged. This is the moment of insights, questions of meaning, doubts and moral requests. Later, M-L. von Franz adds a last step, which is the application of what was confronted to common life. This requires a total acceptance of one's own responsibility.

As in the second stage, the unconscious is the one that takes the lead and the ego becomes a kind of silent interior witness. In the fourth stage, consciousness is the one that takes the lead. This is the moment in which the ego enters actively in the experience (Chodorow, 1997). Active Imagination is a process of dialogue between the conscious and the unconscious and acquires great importance in the process of individuation as a process of differentiation for the development of one's own singularity. In the complexity of this process, Jung develops the concept of "transcendent function". According to Stein (2007), Active Imagination is the most important method to create and activate the transcendent function.

The Transcendent Function

The concept of "Transcendent Function" (Jung, 1916)[8] arose out of Jung's attempt to understand how to come to terms with the unconscious and how to hold the tension of the opposites. He discovered that there is an innate natural process that unifies the opposite positions in the psyche. It attracts polarized energies to a common channel "and creates a living, third thing . . . a living birth that leads to a new level of being, a new situation" (Jung, 1916, para. 189),[9] giving place to a new symbolic position that holds both perspectives at the same time: the emergence of the third. It is not "one or the other" (following the Aristotelian principle of the excluded third, *tertio excluso*) but "both/and", something like a *tertium*, "a third" which in terms of (analytical) logics does not exist, but in the reality of the soul constitutes a living truth. The *tertium datum* holds the tension between the opposites that are related in a co-implication. This places itself within a dialectical, enatiodromic logic (Deligiannis, 2012). The co-existence of the opposites, this paradoxical reality, that includes both, appears as an insoluble conflict in practice. Bárbara Hannah (1998) remembers the importance, in the stage of confrontation, of holding the tension between the opposites.

From the mythical-symbolic point of view, we can think of the image of the god Hermes: as mediator, messenger, conductor, guide of souls that cross the border between life and death. God of liminality and also of creativity, god of crosses, frontiers and "in-between", places that are difficult to inhabit because they generate insecurity, ambiguity, uncertainty, but which are necessary to unite what is separated and to transcend what is dying, living the paradox in order to generate new spaces. Paraphrasing von Foerster (1991), "being able to use paradoxes as creative devices or virtuous circles".

Jung called this function *transcendent* "because it makes the transition from one attitude to another organically possible" (Jung, 1916, para. 145),[10] in such a way that a new attitude can be adopted.

Furthermore, the symbolic function is inseparable from the transcendent function, given that the symbol is the synthetic unit of meaning that encompasses two poles, the manifest and the hidden, bringing together both at the same time and granting new possible meanings according to its plurisignificant character. According to Gordon (1993), the transcendent function is a bridging process at the heart of the capacity to symbolize.

Freedom to Imagine

Active Imagination has been developed by some Jungians and disqualified by others. This has led to certain confusions and misunderstandings about what Active Imagination really is. Moreover, it has been confused with, or assimilated into, different types of visualizations that, without demeriting the importance and utility they have in some determined application fields, interfere with the basic principle of Jungian psychology, which is the relevant autonomous and creative function of the psyche together with the freedom to imagine. James Hillman (1999) insists even more on that, emphasizing:

> The disciplines of the imagination end up disciplining the images, end up mistreating the soul's main freedom: the freedom to imagine . . . we sin against the imagination whenever we ask an image for its meaning, requiring that images be translated into concepts.
>
> (Hillman 1999, pp. 119, 120[11])

For him, images are concrete and refer to special features while concepts are abstract and tend to generalize. The image possesses distinctive qualities, and through these qualities it is possible to find out what is essentially implicit in the image (Adams, 2006).

According to Jung in *Mysterium Coniunctionis*: "Above all, don't let anything from outside, that does not belong, get into it, for the fantasy-image has everything it needs" (Jung, 1955, para. 749).[12] Furthermore, he says: "Image and meaning are identical . . . Actually, the pattern needs no interpretation: it portrays its own meaning" (Jung, 1946, para. 402).[13]

Neuroscience

Generally speaking, images are associated with the visual as we are "visual" animals with more than half of the cerebral cortex dedicated to processing visual information; but some studies (Kobayaschi et al., 2004; Stevenson, 2005) have also explored gustatory and olfactory images, including cenesthetic and kinesthetic sensations (i.e. a movement, a gesture or a posture can generate images) (Deligiannis, 2018). In the same way that thought is bound to language, imagination uses images instead of words; that is to say, we imagine images (Drubach et al., 2007) or they imagine us, without the need of words.

For Chodorow (1994), the nature of imagination, besides being a symbolic process, leads us to the emotional core of complexes. Traumatic experiences in early childhood are usually dissociated and remain captive in the unconscious, in the implicit memory, in the form of complexes (Wilkinson, 2007). These emotionally intense experiences are retained or captured and cannot be verbalized, however they can become present through Active Imagination which allows a direct access to the implicit processes (Wyman-McGinty, 1998) and can establish the relationship between implicit and explicit memory, through the activation of the transcendent function.

From philosophy and cognitive neuroscience, Johnson (1992) suggests that imagination unites the corporeal structures and the cognitive, and that imagination also plays an important role in significance, understanding, reasoning and communication: "Our new ideas and connections come from the imaginative structures that make up our present understanding, from the schemata that organize our experience and serve as the basis for imaginative projections in our network of meanings" (Johnson, 1992, p. 170).[14] Johnson argues that there is no unbridgeable gap between reason and imagination; reason is not disembodied and imagination is indispensable to give sense and meaning to our experience. For Johnson (1992), imagination acts as a bridge between embodied experience and mental conceptualization.

Active Imagination as a method, as a path, more than promote the discharge of emotions in a cathartic way, reveals meanings, heals emotional wounds and enables the emergence of new meanings. Active Imagination may put into action the transcendent function which favors the emergence of new attitudes with properties that did not exist previously or could not have been known before their encounter (Solomon, 2003). Thus, the emergence of new psychological realities capable of reconfiguring the personality (Cambray and Carter, 2004) is facilitated.

Movement as Active Imagination

From all the ways in which Active Imagination is used, I chose Movement as Active Imagination as one of the methods I use in my clinical practice, and it is one of my favorites.

While Active Imagination was developed by Jung, Active Imagination through the body and movement was created by Mary Whitehouse in the 1950s and 1960s and was named "Authentic Movement" or "Movement-in-Depth". Whitehouse was a dancer and pioneer in the field of dance therapy. She studied at the Jung Institute in Zurich and analyzed with Hilde Kirsch in Los Angeles. She integrated her knowledge of the body and movement with Jungian Analytical Psychology and, more specifically, with Active Imagination, to establish a bridge between the unconscious and consciousness. This work was later developed by Janet Adler and Joan Chodorow (a Jungian analyst of San Francisco), who also calls it Movement as Active Imagination or Active Imagination in Movement.

Movement as Active Imagination is done between a person who moves (the mover) and the analyst, who is the witness. The mover starts with her/his eyes closed, paying attention inside, remaining still and silent, waiting for images, sensations, impulses or movements that arise from within and that take shape in a physical action through the body and its movements. Focusing the attention inside and being ready to wait are two basic conditions for this work. As music has a high degree of influence on the inner states, the work is done without music and also without a predetermined plan; it is a non-directive technique. There is no right or wrong way to move (Stromsted, 1998). For Whitehouse (1979), the unconscious is allowed to speak, to make itself visible, when it wants to, while the consciousness observes, is attentive, participating but not directing, cooperating but not choosing.

Attention, to the inner states of the body, bodily sensations and movements, operates as a doorway that opens the connection to pre-verbal stages and primary experiences, bringing the unconscious into consciousness. Forgotten images, some belonging to the collective unconscious (Chodorow, 1994), repressed emotions, traumatic situations, primitive instincts that remain as aspects of the shadow (Stromsted, 2009), vital and deep aspects unknown to the patient, hidden needs, anesthetized talents or restorative images may appear.

The witness/analyst employs a specific quality of attention and presence in the experience of the mover, generating what Kalff (1980) called a "free and protected space". Part of the analyst's task is to act as a support and containment of the mover's (patient's) anxieties, fears or dissociated parts, and to be a witness to the mover's experience. He or she is basically a respectful and empathic observer, resonating with the patient and at the same time paying attention to his or her own feelings, judgments, sensations and impulses to move.

Working with the body allows some meaningful symbols to appear which may contribute to the process of individuation, and enable us to unveil experiences stored in our body that are dissociated from the consciousness. Movement goes directly to the emotional life (Chodorow in Zenoff, 1986), connecting image and emotions (Wyman-McGinty, 1998).

Some Limitations

Despite its advantages and importance in the analytical process, there are situations in which it is advisable not to use Active Imagination.

It is recommended not to apply it at the beginning of a treatment but rather after having done some sessions and having established the therapist/patient bond. In general, it is also not advisable when the patient's ego is not stable enough to withstand the tension of the opposites. At this point it is very difficult to generalize, for which it will be necessary to evaluate in each case the consistency of the patient's ego, the time of treatment, the transferential bond established and the moment of the process. Given these conditions, it can be integrative.

When the consciousness is overwhelmed by many unconscious contents – given that Active Imagination favors the presence of such contents – it is not advisable since the ego can become flooded and psychic disorganization may occur. In spite of this, in some cases it is used to make these contents viable and give them form, thus calming and ordering the psyche. In these situations, the condition is that the ego is sufficiently stable to be able to bear it. For the aforementioned reasons, in the case of borderlines, more directive expressive techniques are recommended.

It should also be kept in mind that the fascination with the contents of the unconscious can operate as a defense that prevents the emotional connection and the integration of these contents in the totality of the psyche.

In the particular case of Active Imagination in Movement, which uses the body as a medium, one of the limitations is that many people show a certain reluctance or refusal to work with the body. On the contrary, if the person has highly developed body work, especially from a discipline such as classical dance, in some cases the emphasis may be placed on the production of a correct or aesthetic movement and be more attentive to the result, to the detriment of the emergence of unconscious movements within a process. In this case, it may be acting as a defense.

A limitation from the therapist's perspective is that the proposal to work with the body implies a different set-up: a physical and spatial displacement, a change of attitude; ultimately it implies leaving the comfort of the armchair.

Finally, although the technique is simple, it works on subtle and deep levels; therefore, one of the observations for the analyst is that he/she should have sufficient knowledge and training in such techniques, together with an ethical attitude.

Clinical Vignette

I have chosen this clinical vignette to exemplify the application of Movement as Active Imagination. Patricia is 41 years old; she is a lawyer and has training in yoga. She likes this more than her job as a lawyer. She would like to dedicate herself totally to yoga, but "I chose to be a lawyer to accompany my dad." She is married, has two children, 9 and 12 years old. Her husband is an engineer, and 70 per cent of the family income depends on her.

She has come into analysis because she wants to work on "situations or structures that emerge at certain moments, which over the years, I polish, interpret, contextualize, but they keep appearing . . . I don't want to get to that point. I don't want to end up exploiting them in a way that I don't want, that I don't like. By not saying 'no' right off the bat, I end up in situations where I feel uncomfortable".

She would like to stop working as a lawyer but she feels that she cannot abandon her father; in the office. "I have to continue accompanying him because I am his daughter." It is very hard for her to think that someone could replace her. She has the feeling of not knowing what to do; duty always prevails over the rest and also her own fears of change.

During the first year of treatment, I suggested working with the body – Movement as Active Imagination – but Patricia did not accept. She said, "I do not give my body at ease, I prefer to work with my mind." I decided to wait a few months until we had established a more trusting relationship. Her first approach to the movement was sensory, cenesthetic; she refers her sensations to the bones, articulations and muscles. Gradually, she was able to break that barrier and her emotions started to show, mingled with visual, olfactory, tactile and kinesthetic images.

Now, I am presenting a session with Movement as Active Imagination in which Patricia connected with the feeling of anger.

After two years and a half of treatment, Patricia came to session saying she would like to work with Movement as Active Imagination because that week a repetitive gesture had appeared that she wished to explore. Then, taking this gesture as a starting point and after a warm up, Patricia looked for a place to start with the experience and she sat on the floor. Some minutes later she put her hands over her eyes, and massaged her face with her fingertips. She then started to swing backward and forward with short movements, as if rocking. She held her head with both hands and tapped it, first with her index finger and then with all her fingers. She held her jaw with her hands and lowered her head (she looked like an angry, capricious girl). Then she tapped her feet on the floor and sat holding her legs, with her arms swinging from side to side (now she looked sad). Sitting with her legs crossed, she put her right hand on her face, swinging and looking restless. Then she played with her hands, moving them up and down, and also from one side to the other as if saying hello, as a girl playing. Slowly, she stood up, gradually pushed with her right hand, and moved forward. She shrugged her shoulders and clenched her fists. After a moment, she stepped with her head forward, opened her hands by her sides and walked.

When the experience was over, Patricia said:

I started from a gesture, which I recently repeated several times: "putting my hands over my face". Soon after, black-and-white photos of myself aged 4 or 5 began to appear. The movements that arose in me were "tantrum like'". I felt like screaming, I was in a whim, I screamed and cried silently . . . I cried because I was not understood . . . I was alone, isolated. I felt calm after I had screamed (silently) . . . for a long time.

Then, a mirror appeared and I began mimicking until the point when I felt like going through it. I was afraid of what I was going to find "on the other side", then I looked back and I saw the room that I had when I was a child.

In this work, Patricia started from a gesture as a kinesthetic image and connected with anger (tantrums, screams), an emotion she felt when she was a child, but which she could not express or process adequately. Anger especially with her mother: "what my mother wanted me to do and I did not want to do. What I was supposed to do, only because I had to, or when I had to take care of my brother, . . . I'm not his mother". Patricia is very angry with her mother but, at the same time, she does not say anything, her anger is hidden and remains in the shadow. She also relates her anger to "I have to", "duty", something she had internalized. "I can't tolerate being wrong." If she makes a mistake, she is afraid of other people's reactions, that the other person may be angry. She said, "there is always something to feel guilty about".

Regarding to the image in the mirror, as a reflection of herself, Patricia said:

> There is a part of myself that I cannot recognize . . . the image I see is me, but not 100 per cent me . . . I feel strange and I am surprised by what I see. It does not respond to my internal register of myself . . . and my exterior image. . . . It is as if my exterior image does not show everything that happens to me.

This is related to my comment that her face shows nothing of what is happening to her, when in fact she is crossed by deep emotions. Her face did not reflect what is happening to her. She said, "I have just realized there is a part of the emotion that is missing." The interior intensity cannot be seen, as it appears as something calm. To the rest of the people she seemed quiet and well balanced. She added, "I have exercised not to show myself." But, inside, there is a register of tension, noise and movement. Part of that interior tension was "a buildup of rage", the muted scream and the unsaid.

During Patricia's analytical process and following the insights produced by this experience with the body movement, we continue working with the theme of anger in the following sessions. The anger was linked to a specific issue: "I don't want to take care of what is not mine . . . I need to look after my space and not be in charge of others' needs." She is aware that what happens to her with her job as a lawyer in her father's office partly is related to satisfying his expectations and needs and not hers. At the same time, it is related to not losing her privileged place, and being accepted and loved by him. Being able to distinguish this and to support the tension in order to achieve her individuation is one of the commitments of this stage of the analysis.

Conclusion

Active Imagination as a method, as a pathway, reveals meanings and restores psychological wounds rather than promoting cathartic discharge of emotions; in other words, it enables the possibility of producing new meanings. It activates the transcendent function in the unconscious, "that curious capacity of the human soul to transform itself' (Jung, 1928, para. 360),[15] an innate function, which operates within the framework of self-regulation and compensation of the psyche, generating a new area of border crossing enabling a new symbolic attitude in the process of individuation.

Images act as a bridge in the psyche: they sometimes bring information and understanding about a state of mind or a symptom, giving them new meaning; at other times they act as a way of elaboration. Intense emotional situations, even those experienced during very early childhood, that cannot be revealed or verbalized, can appear and be told through the moving body. It allows emotions that have been retained or captured to find expression through images before being able to be spoken in words. When the pre-verbal level is activated with Movement as Active Imagination, memories nestling in the unconscious, in the implicit memory, can be accessed, it can cross through defenses and find hidden needs, traumatic situations and anesthetized talents (Deligiannis, 2018).

Lastly, we try to pay attention to the image, to concentrate on it with interest and curiosity and allow the image to speak for itself. Thus, metaphorically, "the vague images of the psyche can be touched with the finger".[16]

Notes

1 Jung, C.G. (1981). *Recuerdos, Sueños y Pensamientos*. Barcelona: Ed. Seix Barral.
2 Jung, C.G. (1926). *Espíritu y Vida*. CW 8. Madrid: Editorial Trotta.
3 Here Jung uses the word fantasy as synonym of imagination.
4 Jung, C.G. ([1921] 1972). *Tipos Psicológicos*. Buenos Aires: Editorial Sudamericana.
5 Geltman, P. (1996). *Gastón Bachelard. La razón y lo imaginario*. Buenos Aires: Editorial Almagesto.
6 Jung, C.G. (1957). *Psicología y Alquimia*. Buenos Aires: Santiago Rueda Editor.
7 Henry Corbin (1972) chooses the word *imaginal* instead of "imaginary" due to the fact that it may confuse with unreal, utopian.
8 It was not published until 1957.
9 Jung, C.G. (1916). La función transcendente. CW 8. Madrid: Editorial Trotta
10 Jung, C.G. (1916). La función transcendente. CW 8. Madrid: Editorial Trotta
11 Hillman, J. (1999). *Re-imaginar la Psicología*. Madrid: Ediciones Siruela.
12 Jung, C.G. (1955/2002). *Mysterium Coniunctionis*. CW 14. Madrid: Editorial Trotta.
13 Jung, C.G. (1946). Consideraciones teóricas acerca de la esencia de lo psíquico. CW 8. Madrid: Editorial Trotta.
14 Johnson, M. (1992). *The Body in the Mind. The Bodily Basis of Meaning, Imagination and Reason*. Chicago and London: University of Chicago Press.
15 Jung, C.G. (1928). La técnica de la diferenciación entre el yo y las figuras de lo inconsciente. CW 7. Madrid: Editorial Trotta.
16 Paraphrasing Henri Bosco (1888–1976) in *L'antiquaire* (1954). Paris: Ed. Gallimard.

References

Adams, M.V. (2006). "Imaginology: The Jungian Study of the Imagination". Article presented at the "Psyche and Imagination" Conference of the International Association for Jungian Studies, University of Greenwich, London.

Cambray, J. & Carter, L. (2004). "Analytic methods revisited". In Cambray, J. & Carter, L. (Eds.), *Analytical Psychology. Contemporary Perspectives in Jungian Analysis* (pp. 116–148). Hove and New York: Brunner-Routledge.

Corbin, H. (1972). "Mundus Imaginalis, the Imaginary and the Imaginal", *Spring*, 72, 1–19.

Chodorow, J. (1994). *Dance Therapy and Depth Psychology. The Moving Imagination.* London and New York: Routledge.

Chodorow, J. (1997). *Jung on Active Imagination.* New Jersey: Princeton University Press.

Dallett, J. (1982). "Active Imagination in practice", in Stein, M. (Ed.), *Jungian Analysis.* La Salle & London: Open Court.

Deligiannis, A. (2012). "Imaginación Activa en Movimiento. Imaginar con el cuerpo en la Psicología Analítica" [Movement as active imagination: Imagining with the body in analytical psychology], in Saiz, M. (Ed.), *Psicopatología psicodinámica simbólico-arquetípica. Una perspectiva junguiana de integración en psicopatología y clínica analítica 3* (pp. 121–143). Montevideo: Prensa Médica Latinoamericana.

Deligiannis, A. (2018). "Imagining with the body in analytical psychology. Movement as Active Imagination: An interdisciplinary perspective from philosophy and neuroscience". *Journal of Analytical Psychology*, 63, 2, 166–185.

Drubach, D., Benarroch, E. & Mateen, F. (2007). "Imaginación: definición, utilidad y neurobiología" [Imagination: Its definition, purposes and neurobiology], *Revista de Neurología*, 45 (6), 353–358.

Geltman, P. (1996). *Gastón Bachelard. La razón y lo imaginario* [Gastón Bachelard: Reason and the imaginary], Buenos Aires: Editorial Almagesto.

Gordon, R. (1993). *Bridges. Metaphor for Psychic Processes.* London: Karnac Books.

Hannah, B. (1998). *Encuentros con el alma: Imaginación Activa como C.G. Jung la desarrolló* [Encounters with the soul: Active imagination as developed by C.G. Jung], Mexico: Editorial Fata Morgana.

Hillman, J. (1999). *Re-imaginar la Psicología* [Re-imagining psychology], Madrid: Ediciones Siruela.

Johnson, M. (1992). *The Body in the Mind. The Bodily Basis of Meaning, Imagination and Reason.* Chicago and London: University of Chicago Press.

Jung, C.G. (1916). *La función transcendente* [The transcendent function] CW 8. Madrid: Editorial Trotta.

Jung, C.G. ([1921] 1972). *Tipos Psicológicos* [Psychological types], Buenos Aires: Editorial Sudamericana.

Jung, C.G. (1926). *Espíritu y Vida* [Spirit and life] CW 8. Madrid: Editorial Trotta.

Jung, C.G. (1928). *La técnica de la diferenciación entre el yo y las figuras de lo inconsciente* [The technique of differentiation between the ego and the figure of the unconscious] CW 7. Madrid: Editorial Trotta.

Jung, C.G. (1946). *Consideraciones teóricas acerca de la esencia de lo psíquico* [The structure and dynamics of the psyche] CW 8. Madrid: Editorial Trotta.

Jung, C.G. (1955/2002). *Mysterium Coniunctionis.* CW 14. Madrid: Editorial Trotta.

Jung, C.G. (1957). *Psicología y Alquimia* [Psychology and alchemy], Buenos Aires: Santiago Rueda Editor.

Jung, C.G. (1981). *Recuerdos, Sueños y Pensamientos* [Memories, dreams, reflections], Barcelona: Ed. Seix Barral.

Kalff, D. (1980). *Sandplay. A Psychotherapeutic Approach to the Psyche.* Santa Mónica, CA: Sigo Press.

Kobayashi, M., Takeda, M., Hattori, N., Fukunaga, M., Sasabe, T., Inoue, N., et al. (2004). "Functional imaging of gustatory perception and imagery: 'topdown' processing of gustatory signals". *Neuroimage*, 23, 1271–1282.

Kugler, P. (1999). "La creación psíquica de imágenes: un puente entre sujeto y objeto" [The psychic creation of images: A bridge between subject and object], in Young-Eisendrath, P. and Dawson, T. (Eds), *Introducción a Jung* [Introduction to Jung], Spain: Cambridge University Press.

Pallaro, P. (2000). *Authentic Movement. Essays by Mary Starks Whitehouse, Janet Adler and Joan Chodorow*. London and Philadelphia: Jessica Kingsley Publishers.

Solomon, H. (2003). "The ethics of supervision: Developmental and archetypal perspectives", in Christopher, E. and Solomon, H. (Eds.), *Contemporary Jungian Clinical Practice*, (pp. 293–308). London: Karnac.

Stein, M. (2007). *El Principio de Individuación. Hacia el desarrollo de la conciencia humana.* [The principle of individuation: Toward the development of human consciousness]. Barcelona: Ediciones Luciérnaga.

Stevenson, R.J. (2005). "Case TI. Olfactory imagery: A review". *Psychonomic Bulletin & Review*, 12, 244–264.

Stromsted, T. (1998). "The dancing body in psychotherapy. Reflections on somatic psychotherapy and authentic movement", in Pallaro, P. (Ed.) (2007), *Authentic Movement: Moving the Body, Moving the Self, Being Moved. A Collection of Essays* (pp. 202–220). London and Philadelphia: Jessica Kingsley Publishers.

Stromsted, T. (2009). "Authentic Movement: A dance with the divine". *Body, Movement and Dance in Psychotherapy: An International Journal for Theory, Research and Practice*, 4(3), 201–213.

Von Foerster, H. (1991). *Las semillas de la cibernética* [The seeds of cybernetics]. Barcelona: Editorial Gedisa.

Von Franz, M.-L. (1982). *C.G. Jung. Su mito en nuestro tiempo* [C.G. Jung: His myth in our time]. Mexico: Fondo de Cultura Económica.

Whitehouse, M. (1979). "C.G. Jung and dance therapy. Two major principles", in Pallaro, P. (Ed.) (2000). *Authentic Movement. Essays by Mary Starks Whitehouse, Janet Adler and Joan Chodorow* (pp. 73–101). London and Philadelphia: Jessica Kingsley Publishers.

Wilkinson, M. (2007). *Coming into Mind. The Mind–Brain Relationship: A Jungian Clinical Perspective.* New York: Routledge.

Wyman-McGinty, W. (1998). "The body in analysis: Authentic movement and witnessing in analytic practice". *Journal of Analytical Psychology*, 43, 239–260.

Zenoff, N. (1986). "An interview with Joan Chodorow", in Pallaro, P. (Ed.) (2000). *Authentic Movement. Essays by Mary Starks Whitehouse, Janet Adler and Joan Chodorow* (pp. 209–228). London and Philadelphia: Jessica Kingsley Publishers.

Chapter 4

Active Imagination and the Psychic Body

Margarita Méndez

It was 1925 in Toni Wolff's consulting room. An analysand – Tina Keller – discovered that she could express herself through movements, letting inner images dance and allowing the use of her body as a resource for Active Imagination. It was the first time they both realized that a feeling could be danced when there are no words for it.

Toni Wolff and Tina Keller witnessed firsthand the emergence and development of Analytical Psychology through their personal relationship with Jung.[1] Wolff was Jung's close collaborator and Keller was a longstanding analysand (1915–1928). Jung's approach to Active Imagination began with his own encounter with the unconscious. Since 1913 Jung had started to note his active imaginations and his reflections about an explanation of the personality; *The Black Books* were on their way (1913–1932, *Notebooks of Transformation*) and they were the genesis of *The Red Book*.

The origin of creative psychotherapies, including the use of the body in movement in Analytical Psychology, may be found in these early stages of Jung's self-investigation from which he elaborated his theory. In 1916 he was going through a deep personal crisis, even though he wrote "The Transcendent Function", which was his first essay on Active Imagination.[2] He described the phenomena of integrating the unconscious to consciousness and how it could lead to an inflation or deflation of the ego by the powerful energies that arise. Through Active Imagination in the course of analysis, those risks of inflation or deflation of the ego, as well as the one-sidedness and critical attitude of the conscious psyche, can be compensated. With time, the blossoming of the creative psyche and of therapeutic reflection could come to light. Eventually these fantasies and the acknowledgment of the creative imagination may open into the process of individuation.

Since then, many analysts have developed the non-verbal dimension of the psyche with an interest that emerged with enthusiasm in the 1960s and 1970s. Among the pioneers who integrated Jungian analysis with the psychic living body (sometimes called Authentic Movement) – and other creative techniques – Joan Chodorow stands out for her comprehensive theoretical and practical approach to the subject, which was expressed in one of her books[3] and many of her writings, the IAAP Pre-Congress Workshops until 2016, and her teachings around the world.

DOI: 10.4324/9781003411383-4

Historically, Active Imagination has had many ups and downs, and in Chiara Tozzi's research presented in this book (see Chapter 1), we can observe that 95 per cent of the analysts and students believe that Active Imagination was relevant in Jung's clinical practice and 90 per cent of training analysts also agree. Such results tend to verify the spread of the knowledge and practice of Active Imagination within the members of the IAAP and that it is possible to give new value to it within our learnings and clinical practices.

To go deeper into our understanding of Active Imagination from my perspective and clinical practice, please allow me to further explore how can we approach the psychic living body in analysis through the archetypes, or should I say through the archetypal image, since the archetype can never be experienced directly – because it inhabits the collective unconscious – and we can have access to it only *via* the archetypal image. Jung's idea was that an archetype can be depicted as a spectrum, ranging from an infrared, physiological or instinctual pole to an ultraviolet, spiritual or imaginistic pole.

For Jung, archetypes were inborn predispositions of the psyche rooted in the instincts which the individual could bring to every level of experience in life. The word archetype comes from the Greek *arche*: archaic and type: pattern. Thus, it is innate archaic patterns and an inherited psychic disposition that enable individuals to react in a human manner.

> Just as, in its lower reaches, the psyche loses itself in the organic-material substrate, so in its upper reaches it resolves itself into a "spiritual" form about which we know as little as we do about the functional basis of instinct.[4]

Jung also described a psychoid level in the psyche which is applicable to almost every archetype. This level expresses the unknown but possible connection between psyche and matter. When Jung applied the notion of archetype to the psychoid unconscious, the psychic/organic link was expressed in the form of a mind–body connection.[5] Joan Chodorow emphasizes that Jung insisted on the contact of the two dimensions in the psychoid:

> Jung proposes the existence of a "psychoid level" which is located in the depths of the unconscious where the two poles in some way meet. The psychoid level functions as a kind of transformative interface between psyche and matter.[6]

The two cones of psyche and matter meet in the vertex of the psychoid area. Jung considered that the psychosomatic phenomena occur in the infrared pole, closer to the instinctual sphere, while the synchronistic ones would be related to the ultraviolet. For a better historical and cultural understanding of the fluctuations from the infrared to the ultraviolet, let's take a look into Hinduism, Kundalini Yoga and the symbolism of the chakras in the body, as they make an excellent example.

A branch of the yoga practices, Kundalini Yoga includes sexual practices and other techniques (breathing, meditation, renunciation) as a way to stop the endless cycle of reincarnations. The term yoga shares its Sanskrit origin meaning yoke in English and *yugo* in Spanish. Kundalini Yoga differs from mainstream Hinduism (which has a strong masculine bias) in that it gives a central role to Shakti, the feminine energy.[7] Due to its emphasis on sexual practices, Kundalini Yoga received literal interpretations and has been misunderstood from the moment it was brought to the West.

Kundalini Yoga consists of consciously awakening the serpent energy that sleeps coiled at the base of the pelvic bone; this process is supposed to awake, one by one, the consciousness related to each of the seven chakras or circles, which are seen as centers of energy located along the spine and from the bottom to the head. The energies of the sleeping serpent begin its chromatic symbolism with the color red at the bottom of the spine and flow to the top of the head, as we might expect, to ultraviolet, and each chakra has its own colors and symbolism.

The sleeping serpent represents the instinctive, the archetypal and collective; if awakened it can lead to a personal path of individuation. Each chakra or center is related to a whole world or level of the human being and the seven centers hypothetically create a subtle body invisible to the eye. The chakras are not only related to the specific part where they are located but to a wide range of experiences in the whole body. Each chakra should be understood as a symbol, *symballein*, a part that can be seen plus an invisible part. In India the chakras represent the planes of a psychological system. The first three chakras are located in the pelvic basin and above the diaphragm there are four other centers. In the first chakras the energy flows upwards and from the fourth circle the movement also becomes horizontal, possibly meaning that it is when the ascent of Kundalini reaches the chest when the connection with "the other" begins and also the empathy among humans.

According to Jung, the symbolic meaning of the experience of the awakened consciousness of each and every chakra begins with Muladhara in the base of the spine (at the rectum), then Swadishtana (sex organs), Manipura (level of the navel), Anahata (near the heart), Vishudha (in the throat), Ajna (between the eyebrows or third eye) and Sahasrara (above the top of the head). The chakras at the pelvis are related to the basic life-sustaining functions: alimentation and eating, sex/procreation and aggression/will of domination.[8] At the next chakra, at the level of the heart, it is supposed that we are able to begin to feel compassion; it is the representation of the beginning of humanity as seen in early hominids when they started caring for and feeding injured members of the group.

The *Muladhara* chakra represents the root, the earth in us, the place for grounding and accepting our destiny. It is also the place where the Gods are asleep. They represent the seeds of what is to come if we want to live the adventure of living and differentiating from the transpersonal. Jung found that this moment can occur quite soon in human life:

As soon as a child notices its body, it feels uncomfortable and cries; it becomes conscious of its own life, of its own ego. . . . Its own life now begins; its consciousness begins to separate itself from the totality of the psyche, and the world of the primordial images, the miraculous world of splendor, lies behind it forever.[9]

In other words, in order to become conscious in the Muladhara world, we have to be expelled from the primordial paradise never to come back again: we must begin to grow at the price of suffering and work, like Adam and Eve.

Swadishtana is related to water and the emotions; the emotions are what really make us individuals. This chakra has to do with differentiating from the mother complex, the sexual instinct and beginning of the tasks of the Psyche. Further on, we will explore the Eros & Psyche's myth, which can be connected with the experiences that inhabit this chakra. This circle can also represents a baptism of water. *Manipura* is associated with fire and the mastering of passions. It is like a baptism of fire and symbolically implies a descent into hell to rescue the treasures that lie there.

Above the diaphragm lies *Anahata* linked to air, the thoughts and the feelings of the heart. It is related to religious feelings, to the coming to reason of passions and with empathy. Then comes *Vishudha*, which is related to ether and the mind. It is the stage of the wise man/woman, the light of knowledge. It is the area of the word, abstract thinking – the cold spheres of thought – and also its pathology: dissociation and schizophrenia. In my clinical experience, this chakra is related to the Kore-Demeter myth and the suffocation often present in the mother and daughter relationship. The expression of feelings through the articulation of words in the verbal cure of psychotherapy and communication in general (also singing), can connect to healing potentials at the level of the throat. Then comes *Ajna*, known as the third eye, and *Sahasrara*, which is the upper cosmic chakra.

According to Jung:

> It is best to understand this by a metaphor. You can imagine the cosmic chakra system as an immense skyscraper whose foundations go deep down in the earth and contain six cellars, one above the other. One could then go from the first up to the sixth cellar, but one would still find oneself in the depths of the earth. This whole cellar system is the cosmic *muladhara*, and we still find ourselves in it even after we have reached the sixth cellar – our personal *ajna*. This we have to keep in mind always, otherwise we fall into the mistake made by theosophy of confusing the personal with the cosmic, the individual light-spark with the divine light. If we do this, we get nowhere, but merely undergo a tremendous inflation.[10]

Jung warned that Western individuals could confuse the collective psyche with the individual one. As I understand it, for him the two last chakras were too far away for the reach of Western man/woman and he said humanity as a whole might indeed be located in *Anahata* or even in *Ajna* at a supra-personal (collective) level, but nonetheless our psychic situation is undoubtedly in *Muladhara*. In order to take care of the individual soul, Analytical Psychology, like yoga, takes into account many archetypes and also allows a path to awaken the psyche from the "sleep of the gods" to a wider consciousness of oneself, opening the gates to a possible individuation. This process should begin with the acceptance of our own emotions (the dark ones and the bright ones) and continue through the recollection of our projections onto the external world, starting in the primordial world of *Muladhara*. Once a person begins the process of differentiation from the images of the collective unconscious, the unfolding of the process may bring the individual either up to the ultraviolet and to the higher elements or down to the infrared, in an upward or downward movement.

In relation to associations with the ultraviolet pole, Jung underlined an epistemological differentiation regarding the meaning of the word "spirit", leaving aside the philosophical and theological discussion. He focused his thoughts on the archetypal imagery of myth, Alchemy and fairy tales. For him the word "spirit" was the non-material aspect of a living person (thought, intention, ideal) as well as an incorporeal being detached from a human body (ghost, shade, ancestral soul). To the alchemists, *spiritus* was a volatile essence, subtle and active, a vivifying agent like the spirit of wine. In German, *geist* is sparkling, enthusiastic or effervescent and it is related to air and breath. A "spirit" is usually winged, active, mobile, stimulating and inspiring, and in each and every archetype the spiritual and vivifying quality can be present.

What has been most remarkable is that Jung realized that yoga techniques are a model of the phases of development of consciousness quite similar to Christian Catholicism in the sense that psychic energy moves from the bottom to the top, from the earthly to the cosmic. The energy that ascends through the chakras could represent the process of transformation of rough matter into psychological substance – from infrared to ultraviolet – in a similar way that a person finds salvation in the elevation of the spirit. In medieval alchemy the same idea takes form in the search to transform vile metals into gold. Jung's achievement was to realize that we owe a great deal to the reconnection with the subterranean forces of the unconscious. Perhaps we need a psychotherapy closer to the Greek god Hermes, a guide to the underworld in a downward movement towards the inside; that would mean a therapy with a psychic attitude rather than a system of an ego-directed attitude. Hermes is a guide to the unconscious and a maker of connections between gods and goddesses, a god of transformation.

And there is where Active Imagination, dream interpretation and the mythic imagination play a crucial role. Why? Because they allow us to build a metaphoric bridge not only between consciousness and the unconscious but between the ego and the archetypes unfolding the layers of the creative unconscious.

In this direction Archetypal Psychology suggested a psychotherapy closer to the mythic images that inhabit the psychic body and allow the many colors of emotional life. Rafael López-Pedraza (1920–2011)[11] stated that Jungian Analysis should appreciate the psyche as a soul, and this suggestion was related to the importance of the feeling function and a warning about the inflation (already pointed out by Jung) relevant when identifying with the upper, aerial, ultraviolet pole.

Rafael López-Pedraza (RLP) expresses his views in more detail in a personal interview published posthumously in 2013:[12]

RLP   To me the psyche is psychological and nothing else, and to be "psychic" means a constant suffering. I take this from the tale "Eros and Psyche" from Apuleius. You can see that all the process of Psyche is to suffer and one is constantly suffering, whether you want it or not.

Margarita Méndez (MM)   *Have your patients stopped suffering?*

RLP   I tell them to keep suffering, but that they learn to suffer. Because suffering from the Ego can produce illness, it can bring serious illnesses.

In this respect, Psyche (in Eros and Psyche's tale) can be an important character because, through her suffering, she manages to transform herself from a mortal maiden to an immortal being so she becomes an archetypal image. Psyche's suffering in performing her tasks, can be seen as a way of growing and counteracting inflation through the integration of dissociated aspects in each and every adventure. She begins to grow stronger and to better understand her own desperation and depression, connecting her body with her emotions that were previously disconnected. López used to pay great attention to the impact of emotional suffering over psychosomatic illness. The possible overcoming of the autonomy of the psyche – represented by Psyche's despair before her tasks and her suicide attempts – can be experienced in the analytical setting in what López called the psychic body. The incorporation of emotions is central in temporarily reaching an integration of dissociative aspects of the psyche that may be trapped in the autonomy of our complexes.

López-Pedraza was a pioneer of Archetypal Psychology, along with James Hillman, Patricia Berry, Valerie Heron, Alfred Ziegler, Niel Micklem and Adolph Guggenbühl-Craig, since the early 1960s in Zurich and London. For him, Analytical Psychology, at that time, needed to progress from the form it took after Jung's death. He felt that Analytical Psychology was becoming more and more polarized towards an emphasis on the ultraviolet pole, so he proposed a reevaluation of what is exclusively psychological. For him, psychotherapy should allow us to approach suffering and pain – either psychic or physical pain – in a "psychic" way, and this should not be identified with the circular suffering of the titan. He suggested that Archetypal Psychology could focus on the emotions in which dreams and images are rooted, and in the psychic body, which is more an experience than a theoretical concept. In psychotherapy, dance and movement can allow a re-connection of the psychic body with the mind, the emotions, the soul, and whatever needs to be reunited in the psyche, because to be rooted in the emotions implies to be rooted in the body.

If we stick to the images that inhabit the chakras, we will find plenty of archetypal images to imagine myths of the body. Also the myths of classical antiquity can provide us with different realms of the body in psychotherapy; for example, Dionysus (who personifies the psychic body) entered the stage of the Greek theater dancing in a ritual madness that was cured and at the same time caused by him; and Hermes with his children, Hermaphrodite, Priapus and Pan (the physical body). And the Maenads, who never felt tired while they danced, sometimes during long periods of time, a feature often shared with Authentic Movement. We can see two types of madness regarding Dionysus: the ecstatic madness that liberates and the tragic madness that is the vengeance of the god. To differentiate these two opposites might bring Dionysus back from his exile, the exile of the psychic body.[13]

The work of Rafael López-Pedraza can help us realize the spectrum of the archetypes that can be felt, thought, intuited and perceived in the psychic body of the analysand and the analyst. The whole range of emotions can be expressed which goes from the infrared physical-biological body rooted in the instincts to the ultraviolet or spiritual pole. López doesn't refer to Active Imagination as a tool or technique; he would rather approach the psychic body in psychotherapy to compensate the conscious psyche with its healing potentials. In order to integrate post-Jungian perspectives with the use of the body and movement in Active Imagination, we have to encourage workshops and seminars on the myths of the body since the mythic imagination can serve as a bridge to spontaneous expression.

Active Imagination, dreams and mythic imagination are three rivers that run parallel in the psyche and might communicate between each other at any time. It is important to be aware that in Active Imagination the images that emerge cannot be suggested by the mover or the witness (therapist) of the movements; they arise from the depths in a completely creative and genuine way.

Following this perspective, I had the opportunity to find images for workshops in the vast archetypal symbolism of religions, fairy tales, myths, body symbolism and dreams such as: the bones, the hymns of Innana, Psyche and her four tasks, Perseus and the gorgon, Hansel and Gretel, Prometheus thief of fire, chaos and rebirth, Mandala, the house and the body, the temple of the earth, cultural complexes and conflict in the body, and more.

In the exploration of the kernel of the expression of the unconscious, Joan Chodorow and Rafael López-Pedraza shared an interest in taking forward and developing Jung's legacy. López deeply appreciated that his considerations about a psychotherapy ruled by the ancient god Pan were an inspiration for Chodorow's reflections about the practice of therapy through dance in one of her articles:

Since the early days, psychoanalysis has been known as a "talking cure". But underlying the process of verbal dialogue and exchange is the ongoing, continuous dialectic of expressive movement. This deep, non-verbal level is fundamental to the success of psychotherapy. In his discussion of Pan/Echo López-Pedraza (1977) weaves wonderfully rich images around a therapy based on Echo-like reflections.[14]

The happening of Pan's echo in psychotherapy can constellate a true epiphany of Pan, which is one of the most vivid expressions of the psychotherapeutic relationship, *similia similibus curantur*[15] . . . this is where the real symmetry happens, where the dance is, where the psychotherapy of Pan is. It is the expression of two bodies dancing in unison, a psychotherapy of the body. Are we in the psychoid realm? Perhaps – but for sure we are in the realm where Pan appears in a psychotherapy within a sort of dance and through body movements, constellating the transference which belongs to him.[16]

The activation of the psychic body promotes psychic movement[17] and whenever we try to understand the psychic living body, the God Pan – who was in Dionysus' cortege – appears like the missing link between the somatic and instinctual pole and the psychic or intuitive pole of our body–psyche system.

To conclude, we can extend bridges with our inner world and dreams with the help of Active Imagination and the mythic imagination. The body holds its own reasons and secrets and they could be unveiled to discover a body inhabited by Dionysus (a metaphor of the repressed emotional and psychic body), perhaps the most repressed of the Greek gods along with Pan, and they demand to be recognized.[18] Dionysus and what he represents had been condemned to exile by religion and culture taking away from us centuries ago the meaning of his initiation rites which we are no longer able to decode. The signals, intensity and limits of a body capable of feeling and expressing emotions comprise what we might call a psychic body; it is an animated body, full with anima, animated by Psyche. The emotional psychic body present in psychotherapy shows up and imposes itself, demanding a life in colors – not in black and white – from the infrared to the ultraviolet.

Notes

1 Oppikofer, R. "Tina Keller. Her fascinating and creative work inspired by the psychology of C.G. Jung". *Jung Journal: Culture & Psyche*, 9(1). C.G. Jung Institute, San Francisco, 2015, 56–62.

2 Jung, C.G., "The Transcendent Function", in the *Collected Works of C.G. Jung* (vol. 8). Princeton University Press, Princeton, New Jersey, 1969/78.

3 Chodorow, J. (Ed.) *Jung on Active Imagination.* Encountering Jung Collection, Princeton University Press, Princeton, New Jersey, 1997.

4 Jung, C.G., in the *Collected Works of C.G. Jung*, CW 8, par. 380, p. 183, 2nd edn, 1969, Bollingen Series XX, Princeton University Press, Princeton, New Jersey.

5 Samuels, A., Shorter, B. and Plaut, F. *A Critical Dictionary of Jungian Analysis*, Routledge, New York & London, 1986, p. 122.

6 Chodorow, J. *Dance Therapy & Depth Psychology*, Routledge, New York & London, 1991. p. 44.

7 Jung, C.G. *The Psychology of Kundalini Yoga*, notes of a seminar given in 1932, Shamdasani, S. (Ed.), *Bollingen Series XCIX*, Princeton University Press, Princeton, 1996, p. xxii.
8 Campbell, J. *The Power of Myth* with Bill Moyers, Doubleday, New York, 1988. p. 173.
9 Jung, C.G. "Psychological Commentary on Kundalini Yoga", *Spring Journal* (1976), p. 31.
10 Jung, C.G. *The Psychology of Kundalini Yoga*, Notes of the seminar given in 1932, Shamdasani, S. (Ed.), Bollingen Series XCIX, Princeton University Press: Princeton, 1999, p. 68.
11 Rafael López-Pedraza was a Cuban-born Venezuelan psychotherapist who studied Analytical Psychology in the C.G. Jung-Institute in Zurich for 11 years and returned to Caracas in 1974. He was an individual member of IAAP, *Doctor Honoris Causa* of the *Universidad Central de Venezuela* in 2009 and author of nine books translated into many languages. The Vol I of his Collected Works was published in Spanish and it include his first three books: *Hermes and his Children, Cultural Anxiety* and *Dionysus in Exile.*
12 *Revista Venezolana de Psicología de los Arquetipos*, 5: 66–67.
13 López-Pedraza, R. *Vol I Obra Reunida*, Pre-Textos, Valencia, 2021.
14 Chodorow, J. "Dance/Movement and Body Experience in Analysis", in Pallaro, P. (Ed.), *Authentic Movement: A Collection of Essays by Mary Starks Whitehouse, Janet Adler and Joan Chodorow*. Jessica Kingley Publishers, London and Philadelphia, 1999, p. 255.
15 *Similia similibus curantur*: "like cures like" principle.
16 López-Pedraza, R. *Hermes and His Children*, Zurich, Switzerland, Spring Publications, 1977. pp. 84–85.
17 Raydán, P. "Cuerpo Psíquico" [Psychic body] http://svaj.net/publicaciones/pablo-raydan-cuerpo-psiquico/
18 Villalobos, M. "Cuerpo Psíquico" [Psychic body] http://svaj.net/publicaciones/magaly-villalobos-cuerpo-psiquico/ in http://svaj.net/

Chapter 5

A Rite of Passage
Interview with Elsa Piperno

Chiara Tozzi

The content of this chapter is based on the words of dancer, choreographer, and teacher Elsa Piperno, who kindly accepted to be interviewed by Chiara Tozzi on Active Imagination.

Phase 1: Emptying/Letting Things Happen

When I was just a little girl, I used to tell other girls to go to the barre so I could teach them something I probably did not even know yet! I really liked to express myself freely, to improvise, and, in some way, those were the first steps to my becoming a dancer, a choreographer, and a teacher. Depending on what I am doing, my approach to dance changes. For example, when I rehearse, I am more rational, but when I get on stage, I completely let myself go.

I really believe in the strength of movement and in analyzing everything around me. Ever since I was young, I have always dreamed a lot; I always believed in my dreams and I tried to understand them. I also had some recurring dreams. With my modest abilities, I tried to grasp the messages behind them. I remember my father used to tell us about his dreams every morning. It was incredible! Each artist needs to find their own way of expressing themselves and get rid of frills; it is easier if you know the technique. Nowadays, techniques are often rejected but I think they are necessary if you truly want to let go. You obviously need more than just the technique, but without the basic knowledge you are much more limited in your expressive capacity. Through movements and dance I was able to discover many things about myself. In some way I changed, and this was functional to my desire and curiosity to grow as a dancer. I have always had a strong personality and at times others tried to take advantage of me. At some point, I decided to stand up for myself and I took this into my teaching and my choreographies. I shared it with my dancers. It is easy for others to label you if you have a strong personality, if your movements are sharp, angular, and direct. I started studying everything I could, even beyond the Graham technique, which is strong and therefore perfect for my personality. I started realizing that to become a full-round artist I also needed to express things that went beyond myself as a dancer. But first I had to be the one to learn and understand them, to then transform them into movements and dance.

DOI: 10.4324/9781003411383-5

When I rehearse a choreography, I start by analyzing everything I have to do: the parts and the relation with others, the quality of the movements, the dynamics, the music or sound in general. In some way, to rehearse is to rationally collect information, and the longer you rehearse, the better the result will be.

You need to step away from rationality to have a relationship with the audience, the other whom you do not see but you know exists. When you are on stage, you are not rational anymore, you are at another level. *The dancer inside me completely empties herself.* For me – and it is not the same for everyone – the dancer inside me definitely corresponds to the first phase of active imagination.

At some point in my career, I realized I was too tolerant. I was accepting a sort of emotional blackmail that did not help me nor others. Sometimes – not often – based on the emotions I was feeling, I got very upset. This is not acceptable, because if you are teaching you need to understand what is going on, and you should always find a way to solve the problem without getting upset. I was able to transform the way I felt when something was not going as I had hoped, and I changed my approach. Not from a creative point of view – even though, of course, creativity is part of teaching, there is no doubt about that; it is the other parallel level. When you teach, you experience things differently than when you are dancing or preparing a choreography. When you are teaching you are rational, you are present. Yet, when I am teaching, something incredible happens – be aware, what I am about to say may make me sound schizophrenic! When I teach an exercise, through a canonical exercise – which follows the same structure for all but is adapted depending on the dancer – or by showing a movement or a combination that I am creating in that moment, I am rational. But apart from that logical moment, when the exercise starts and I see it, I let go and I completely empty myself, and that is when I see all the images that I pass on to others. Through what I see, I come up with certain images which also have to do with what the dancers are doing, and therefore I explain, and it all comes very naturally.

The act of emptying before dancing is like a rite of passage and, in some way, it is sacred.

When I do my makeup just before a show, I completely empty myself and, in some way, I kill a part of who I am. I am not the same person who wakes up in the morning and does her makeup to go run some errands. No, I do my makeup and, in that sacred moment, I detach from myself and I enter into a whole new world.

Everyone in my company knew how special that moment was for me. In fact, whenever we had a show, I did not care to get the most beautiful dressing room, it just had to be isolated. Everyone else was loud and I did not want to hear them! Nobody would dare to ask me for a black eyeliner or a lipstick, they knew it would make me go crazy! At times, this made me look like a snob. Once I was on a show with the famous Italian soprano Katia Ricciarelli. I was there to dance, she was there to sing, but we had not met before the show. After rehearsing, someone knocked on my door and said: "Elsa, Katia is here to say hi." Cold as ice, I replied: "Later." I did not care who was there to see me, I was not available. It was very important for me to take that special moment to do my makeup and detach from my everyday self.

Phase 2: Accepting the Irrational and Incomprehensible

I did some Tai Chi and, even though it was not for long, it was a very important experience. Thai Chi is the opposite of the Graham technique. In Tai Chi there are infinite combinations, the movement never stops, it is very slow; the complete opposite of who I am. I go from an attack to a suspension, then I hold a position, and then again I go up and down. Having to tell my body and my mind to learn this new movement was shocking but also enriching. It helped me understand we are full of resources and we have it all within ourselves. Life, experiences, DNA, where we are born, all have an influence on who we are, but in the end, we can do and become anything we want.

Some choreographers get on stage, they see the dancers, and they immediately create. I am not like that, I need time to think, and this usually happens when I am on my sofa, staring at the ceiling, in a state of contemplation. That is when I am able to alienate myself from the everyday routine. Once I identify the choreography, I move on to looking for sounds, I read books, I allow myself to be impressed by colors. It is very important for me to give myself this time. I need to know how I want to start and finish a choreography. Things may change, I do not always end my choreographies as I had imagined, but I still feel the need to know. I feel more at ease knowing how I want to finish, knowing what the message will be, knowing what I want to tell the audience. *Every time I prepare a choreography, there is always a moment when I am alone and I experiment freely based on my previous thoughts and ideas. I try the steps, I improvise, I go with the flow that comes from within.*

Phase 3: Recording of Images Transforming Themselves

I use my body to express myself, so what better way than to start from the basics, like breathing? I have always had an interest in philosophy, technique, the concept of art according to Martha Graham. In some way, I have it easy. Everything Martha did, her dance technique, starting from breathing, has to do with our inner self and how everything starts from within to come out in a dialectical method. She brilliantly started from the most elemental movements of contraction and release, therefore a dialectic that leads you to see the movement in the dynamic. Yoga also focuses on breathing but it is more static than dance and Martha Graham's technique. Now it is easier because you can record yourself, but I remember back in the days there were times when I was so into the choreography, I would forget what I was creating. When you are the choreographer, you not only need to find the right movement; you also need to pass it on to others, which is the hardest part. When you walk into a theater, you bring along what you imagined, what you created, and you need to see how the dancers will react. As a teacher, I always explain what I am doing and dancers like knowing what I expect from them, what I want to express and communicate. Some choreographers just tell dancers what to do without explaining their thoughts but I believe the greatest part is that you have to do with another body, another mind, another psyche; your movement must adapt and transform itself. It is incredible, very often enriching. You teach a movement and the dancer gives it back with something even more intense. That same movement changes: it is like a daughter or a son, it steps away from what you created, you are not the one deciding anymore. The choreography has your DNA but it also has something of its own. You see your work go beyond what you had imagined.

I never transferred a dream or a vision of a dream into a choreography. But some dreams really shed light on my behaviors, thoughts, or ways of facing life and reality, and this obviously transferred into my work. As previously mentioned, I carried out a "homemade analysis". I did not have all the resources, but I read books, I was curious. Following Martha Graham, it could not have been any other way! She lived during the historical period of psychoanalysis, and this is present in many of her choreographies. You cannot ignore it if you want to be a part of that world. You must learn more through reading. This helped me differentiate between what appeared in my dreams because I had experienced it in my everyday life, and something deeper, belonging to a past from far away. I faced it all with my "homemade approach", but it was very helpful. Yet, there is no movement that comes from a dream. From an emotion, yes, but not from a vision.

Learning things about myself is always an incredible and gratifying experience. It helps me understand that no matter the limits we may set for ourselves in our relationship with others, there are some limits we overcome without even realizing it and this, I believe, is extraordinary.

When I completely empty myself, I am able to see all the images I pass on to others. I often use cooking metaphors in my lessons, it is my way of explaining a contraction or what a dancer may be doing wrong. I try to explain it is not a matter of looks but substance. I often use the metaphor of the egg: if you eat your eggs sunny-side up or soft-boiled you can see the egg; but if you eat egg pasta you know the egg is there although you cannot see it. If the egg were not there, the past would taste differently, and the same applies to mayonnaise, etc. When students hear this metaphor they immediately understand because they see it, and seeing it allows them to build bridges, it makes everything easier. This has always come natural to me, I never had to study it. Today, just like 40 or 50 years ago, I am very grateful for having been blessed with this resource that is not only beautiful but also very rewarding. Losing it would be a tremendous loss. Over the years, my body has changed, and this is very painful for someone like me who spent her whole life dancing. But I am left with something incredible and shocking. In all my lessons, there is always a moment when I see others and I enter into a world of images, fantasy, imagination. A world that allows me to tell them what I expect from them and how I think they can get there in the easiest possible way.

Phase 4: Ethical Comparison

After seeing my choreographies, some people have come to me to ask me if I was intentionally trying to show a certain aspect about myself. Every time, I was caught off-guard and I realized that the choreography had revealed parts of who I am. *Through movements, through my creative honesty, I ended up putting myself out there beyond what I had planned.* What I call honesty related to dance, art, my artistic self, means never wanting to cheat. The more experience you have, the easier it is to cheat. With experience, you may be able to create a choreography in just one week: you choose four movements that go good together in a more or less engaging choreography, and you are done. I never have and never will do this. I have always experimented and tried to go beyond the sole Graham technique, which I have always taught like I think it should be taught, never trying to make it "more modern". I did not want to give in to thinking that the technique was old and outdated and that people are looking for something different. It was hard but I never gave in because I believe in it and because, just like you, many others have told me that their dance experience is vital in their work, even though what they do has nothing to do with dance. Yet, applying what they learned helps them make sense of things. This, I believe, is honesty: not to use the mental resources that come from wisdom and experience to transform reality into something else.

It is very hard to put the concept of "creative honesty" into words, but I will try. Imagine you go see a show and after 5 minutes you start yawning and want to leave. In that case, you know the show is not authentic and the message is not coming across. Thank God people can feel this, even though they may not have the courage to say so. Very often people have come up to me after a show to ask for my opinion: if I have the courage to say the show was incredibly boring, they also admit they did not enjoy it. I think that having a reaction, whether positive or negative, means someone is communicating something, and when someone communicates their truth, you know the show is real, even though you may still decide to walk away. But if you get bored and cannot keep your eyes open, it means there is nothing on the other side, and at that point you may get upset because you might as well be doing something else. You may have even spent money on that ticket. It is unacceptable! Many years ago I went to see a show by Lucinda Childs, a great American choreographer and, at the time – things may have changed after that – her choreography was marked by repetition, like a circle that kept turning. I got very upset because I thought she was making fun of the audience. I was very angry, I wanted to leave, but I decided to stay and that is *when I started to realize that if someone gives you something to think about, it means they are being honest.*

I have many positive memories that may help me better explain what I mean by "creative honesty". Meeting Martha Graham was one of my highest moments. It was love at first sight. When you fall in love so deeply, you feel like you could die right then as you experienced something so incredible and rare. I fell in love with Martha when I saw her on stage for the first time at the Edinburgh festival. It was 1963, the year I got married, and that was my wedding gift. I demanded tickets to the show because I felt like I absolutely had to go see her. She was at the Edinburgh festival for one week and I went to see her the whole time she was there! I had seen a video of her and it had shocked me, I knew I had to see as many of her choreographies as possible, therefore I bought tickets for the afternoon and the night shows.

I got a headache after every show because watching her dance was so incredible, it was true authenticity, transfer through everything I could see: the costume, the movements, the set, the music. Everything touched me deeply and incredibly. On my last day there, I had tickets to see the afternoon show and, right after that, I had to fly back home for the wedding. I could not miss that last show! So I went to the theater, I left my suitcase in the checkroom and asked the usher to please come get me at a certain time because I had to fly back home to go get married. She looked at me as if I were crazy! When she came to tell me it was time, I was on the balcony and I left walking backwards as I had to grasp every last moment of the show. I could not take my eyes off the stage! This is authenticity. This is creative honesty. I also experienced it other times in my life, but only with the greatest. Some artists are blessed with a gift, and they have a huge power. For example, I experienced it with Rudolf Nureyev, when he had just left Russia, at the beginning of his career, and all that time up to Margot Fonteyn. It was incredible! I fell in love when I saw *Le Noces* by Bronislava Nijinska, the younger sister of Vaslav Nijinsky, the author of one of the best choreographies I have ever seen. Just imagine how I felt when I saw her on stage! I saw her many times after that. Some shows really express their intellectual honesty, true creativity. For example, I could never teach like Alwin Nikolais because his technique is foreign to me, but his shows truly impressed me, I could see everything and more, my brain was racing!

I believe all this complex journey that ends in the final performance, and can definitely be compared to the four phases of Active Imagination, reveals the true and final meaning of dance.

Once you are on stage, you cannot control what happens. You are only in control of what you collected and elaborated over time. If something unexpected happens, having more experience helps you more easily solve the problem. For me, if something goes wrong, the show is ruined, I experience it differently. When I was in charge of directing my company, I was not simply a dancer like the time I was with the London Contemporary Dance Theatre. I remember I was always worried about something. More than once a spotlight did not work, and when this happened my mood changed and I would mess up a movement. I was at a different level of the brain. This did not only happen to me when I was a dancer, because, in that case, I was far from being rational. And dancing, I sometimes felt like everything was perfect.

Other times I felt like everything was perfect, everything came easy to me, as if I were outside my own body and I could communicate with the audience.

The energy kept flowing back and forth, from me to them, from them to me. This usually only happens for a moment of a show, but if it happens for an entire choreography, you know you are in heaven!

Figure 7 Elsa Piperno.

Chapter 6

Active Imagination and Painting

Four Phases to Represent the Possible Similarities and Figurative Expression

Luca Padroni

First there is a dream then the awakening. In the awakening the emptying, emptiness, something that you don't quite understand what it is. I wait, I take time, patiently. In the non-movement I let something take shape: a color, a sound, a threat. If I run away I don't move. If I move I fly. Something in the image trembles: is it the idea? I almost close my eyes, I make the dead man afloat, I open my fingers well, my palms upwards: I receive.

Figure 8 Cachoeira, watercolor on paper, 42 × 60 cm, 2022: Gray, light blue, green and black abstract shapes on a white background.

DOI: 10.4324/9781003411383-6

Is the hand free, does the hand have the talent or is it the talent? The hand welcomes what it does not see, what it does not understand, what it can achieve without the use of intellect, reasoning, reason. The physical component remains at the mercy of inner fury, I let free the archaic and anarchist power, the incomprehensible claim to tell the world, a hidden lust for knowledge.

Figure 9 Cachoeira, watercolor on paper, 42 × 60 cm, 2022: Gray, blue, green and black abstract shapes on a white background, with tree and vegetation sketched on the left.

Imagination, fantasy act as destructive propellants – as creators destroyers – towards the image that was previously built in the head: the body – myself, author creator painter – delimits the contours of vision: it builds a castle around a crumbly taste of emptiness. What will happen? Nobody knows that.

Figure 10 Cachoeira, watercolor on paper, 42 × 60 cm, 2022: Gray, green and black vegetation, with a tree on the left and white waterfalls.

In art everything is amoral, above ethics and morality. The artistic gesture reveals its objectivity in its fulfillment. Every attitude is ethical first of all towards oneself.

Figure 11 Cachoeira, watercolor on paper, 42 × 60 cm, 2022: Green and black vegetation with a tree on the left, white waterfalls and details of leaves.

Chapter 7

The Experience of Grace

The Possibility of Transformation in Vladimir Nabokov and Carl Gustav Jung[1]

Chiara Tozzi

To summarize and highlight the meaning and main points of their analytical path, most of my patients described their perception of the transformation experienced in the course of their treatment with the following images: a confused and painful beginning that progressively turns into a wider, clearer and more populated horizon. Their own suffering became progressively more tolerable; and in direct proportion, their curiosity about people and events around them increased. "The memory I have of the first time I sat in this chair," says a patient, "is just of myself. In my memory of that first session, there is a sort of dark well, populated only by grief; it was as if I could not see either you, doctor, or the stuff in your office, but only my terrible face which, I was sure, reflected the horror which gripped me and from which I yearned to be free. Only over the weeks, the months and the years which followed have I begun to 'realize, to see and to hear' the rest of the things, here and outside."

Almost all reports show this trend: the experience of a possible well-being, albeit difficult to focus on a single point as its genesis, is accompanied by the perception of a *quid*: something difficult to put into words but felt fully during particularly emotional sessions where, in the words of the patients themselves, "the deepest point has been touched" . . . "a connection is made between the events described and their feelings" and "their own way of being has been found and taken up". I agree with some of my patients' perceptions and definitions of the essence of transformation as something that can be seen as a possible *state of grace*, a condition which is, at the same time, a psychological, emotional and existential link between the conscious and the unconscious, between themselves as individuals and the world around them, an unexpected gift and a difficult experience to explain. Understanding is only possible through symbolic manifestations, such as art or the sharing of ritual forms. The exercise of active imagination, as experienced and practiced by C.G. Jung and wonderfully illustrated in the *Red Book*, is a creative and illuminating synthesis of this form of experience. But how can we explain, without too much complexity, the features of this process of individuation? The very definition of "technique" to achieve this goal, commonly used to describe active imagination, is highly simplified and seems unsatisfactory and incorrect – as pointed out by Gerhard Adler – in the same way that no one could speak of a "technique of dreaming" (Adler, 1966). It seems more appropriate to use the word

DOI: 10.4324/9781003411383-7

"attitude", as Adler did, to define the paradoxical "active passivity" whereby many people meet what emerges from their unconscious, an attitude described by Adler as similar to that experienced by the beholder of a movie or a listener to music (Adler, 1966).

In both cases, you sit and "receive" something that is not produced by the viewer or listener, but which *happens* and whose deeper meaning can be experienced only through a very specific form of activity. The only difference – says Adler – is that in active imagination, the "film" is created and projected inside oneself.

Both in my work as an analyst and as a writer and writing and script-writing professor, I have found that individuative and creative well-being comes from the ability to profoundly assume this different attitude to observe, experience and live, with the same degree of affection, both the "inner film" of one's psychic life and the "outer film" of everyday life and the real world we live in. This allows us to detect details and curiosities, and to perceive beauty, as well as connections which sometimes surprise us, and that pain and habit usually tend to reduce or hide completely. Both with my students in creative writing and psychology courses and in my work as an analytical psychotherapist, I have found it very useful to explicitly refer to the story by V. Nabokov, *Beneficence*[2] (Nabokov, 1924) for its metaphorical and symbolic ability to "explain" the transformation I am referring to. I must say that while reading Nabokovian fiction, I did and still keep detecting a creative and psychological affinity with C.G. Jung's narrative, especially when this narrative concerns some "life stories", both autobiographical and of the patients. This style, whether in Nabokov or Jung, is closely connected to the content, and makes it possible to notice many notable and interesting affinities. Jung's language is almost always symbolic: "The language I speak must be ambiguous, must have two meanings, in order to do justice to the dual aspect of our psychic nature," said Jung in 1952 (Jung, 1961). Perhaps much of the fascination and power of his message is due precisely to this double level, which could be defined as a "subtext" both from a psychological and literary point of view. For his part, Nabokov, with the double, if not multiple layering of narrative levels, is certainly a master. The labyrinth of mirrors he is able to create with his storytelling is quite prestigious. The objects and characters of his narrative, the narrator and the reader, as well as the plot, are doubled, exchanged, mirrored and faceted with acrobatic grace, making us sink into a narrative reality very similar to that of dreaming and imaginative fairy tales. Even more than in the famous *Lolita*, his novels *The Gift* (1963), *Transparent Things* (1972) and *The Real Life of Sebastian Knight* (1941) are vivid proof of his extraordinary talent. My keen interest in the works of these two great masters has led me to discover how the dominance and wise clarity through which both Jung and Nabokov master this psychological and communicative duplicity originates from a surprising affinity we could call "formative" in both of them. The narration through which Jung reconstructs his early childhood, his family relationships, and his progressive relationship with the world in *Memories, Dreams, Reflections* (Jung, 1961, Cap. I and II), has much in common with what Nabokov gives us in his autobiography *Speak, Memory* (Nabokov, 1966); the special and affective manner of playing through the images of everyday reality and interpreting, processing and reconstructing them in both a subjective and objective, visionary and literal way seems to have been a quality they both shared since childhood. A strong intuition and early opportunities to experience events and links which are difficult to explain through logic and sensory experience are part of their autobiographical memory. Those particular fantasies, which allowed a young Jung to see the picture with the portrait of an ancestor come to life and act (Jung, 1935), and would lead him to the exercise of active imagination as an adult, are matched by the fascinating childhood "visions" of Nabokov, who describes his experience as follows:

> How far as do my memories of myself reach [. . .]. I have been subjected to mild hallucinations [. . .]. They come and go, without the participation of the sleepy observer, but they differ essentially from dream images, since he is still master of his senses.
>
> (Nabokov, 1966, p. 30)

This experience, common to both of them as children, is positively reinforced by a similar response by their own mothers. Like Jung, Nabokov tells us how his mother accepted with serenity some of his childhood experiences of precognition and parasensorial perception, stating that she also had and still experienced similar events. "Oh yes – she would say as I mentioned this or that unusual sensation. Yes, I know all that" (Nabokov, 1966, p. 36). As an adult, commenting on his mother's approach, Nabokov said:

> Her intense and pure religiosity took the form of her having equal faith in the existence of another world and the impossibility of comprehending it in terms of earthly life. All one could do was a glimpse, amid the haze and chimeras, something real ahead, just as people with an unusual persistence of diurnal cerebration is able to perceive in their deepest sleep, somewhere beyond the throes of an entangled and inept nightmare, the ordered reality of the waking hour.
>
> (Nabokov, 1966, p. 37)

The affinity of experience with an open and curious attitude toward what is not usual and empirically demonstrable seems, both for Jung and Nabokov, to relate to that particular "permeability of the membrane between the conscious and the unconscious" (Jung, 1957, par. 134). Jung defined it as the advantage and specific feature of creative people who, more than others and thanks to that very permeability, are capable of tapping in to that huge container of psychic energy and universal images that is the collective unconscious, and to translate this collective evocation of the "archetypal experience" into a symbolic language. Nabokov poetically reaffirms the same observation, arguing that:

> There is, it seems, in the dimensional scale of the world, a kind of delicate meeting place between imagination and knowledge; a point at which great things are reduced and small ones are enlarged in a way which is inherently artistic.
>
> (Nabokov, 1966, p. 24)

Apart from evoking the Jungian concept of synchronicity as a possible link between matter and the psyche, a similar openness to the unthinkable but "imaginable" possibilities of life seems to unite Nabokov and Jung in their dedicated search for relevant connections that give meaning to human existence. It is amazing to notice that while Jung defines this existential goal that can transform the way we perceive and live our lives as "individuation" (Jung, 1946–47, par. 400), Nabokov states in almost identical terms that "The following of such thematic designs through one's life should be, I think, the true purpose of autobiography" (Nabokov, 1966, p. 24).

Although conducted through different disciplines and methods, the life and works of Jung and Nabokov – allow me to emphasize that Nabokov repeatedly manifested his aversion to anything that had to do with psychoanalysis and in particular with the theories of S. Freud (Nabokov, 1973)! – are also characterized by an attitude of confidence regarding *whatever can happen*, which seems to be supported not only by logic, but by an almost religious devotion, evident in Jung's words when he states: "The grace of God indicates a particular state of mind in which I meet with fear and doubt the future, animated by the intense hope that everything will end well" (Jung, 2009, pp. 102–103). This seems to have something to do with the abandonment and receptivity to the experience of grace that we can all experience through living, creating, working.

"How strange, Doctor . . . – said after a few years of analysis a patient who struggled to free himself from the leaden chains of skepticism and depression due to the absolute predominance of his thinking function – change through analysis can be achieved only if you believe in it . . . believe in it even when you think it is the most incredible thing!"

In fact, when patients come to our office, the energy directed to the symptom that brings them to us makes them inert, blind, deaf and often anaffective towards the sense of their individual history and the collective history to which they belong. Just like for the protagonist of Nabokov's story *Beneficence*, which I will refer to to try to explain the "amazing" but possible individuative transformation of Jungian Psychology.

The story begins with an image that is both visual and narrative. We are in Berlin, at dawn, and a man is sitting on a wicker chair. Behind him, a backdrop drawn on canvas lilac, with a fragment of a balustrade, a whitish urn and a hazy garden. The man has been sitting there all night, thinking about a woman whose presence is important in his life, not only in the thoughts that have kept him awake, but also in his work. We come to learn he is a sculptor and that his work, lately, is centered on the image of a woman, probably in clay, whose female figure begins to materialize:

> Roughcast clay heads gradually floated out of the mark into the dusty haze. One of them (your likeness) was wrapped in a wet rag.

The man discovered that the woman betrayed him. He demanded an explanation which was not forthcoming. Therefore, the two did not see each other for two weeks. Then, unable to resist, he called her and made an appointment that afternoon at the Brandenburg Gate. The man only has one goal, one thing to accomplish: to win back the woman he loves. But there is another man. Someone who stands between him and her, who prevents our hero from getting total possession of his woman; that fusional and symbiotic possession which would allow him to be calm and not feel so bereft of dignity as to laugh at himself. Reading the story both from the narrative and the psychological point of view, we could say the man is suffering from a love obsession. This obsession is crippling and exhausting, both psychologically and physically. He is wondering who he is, what he wants and why he is suffering so much. The answer he finds, that is to say, the *meaning* of his life apparently lost, is – he seems convinced – very simple: he wants to be loved by *this* woman, a *liar* and a *savage*; he wants to hear her voice, so *distant and restless*. When the protagonist of the story is presented to us, his self-awareness and the *meaning* of his life are limited and circumscribed by the obsession of his love.

> I spoke to you with tight eyes, and felt like crying. My love for you was the throbbing, welling warmth of tears. That is exactly how I imagined paradise: silence tears, and the warm silk of your knees. This you could not comprehend.

Isn't this the state of mind most people find themselves in when they are about to start therapy? Paralyzed by a shortcoming and/or by a symptom. Unable to make sense of their days, their work, their dreams. Dominated, *possessed*, to put it in Jungian terms, by a *complex*. And, therefore, with their narrow, claustrophobic and demotivating awareness and horizons.

Even Carl Gustav Jung, after the agonizing visions and dreams experienced between October 1913 and the summer of 1914, lived in a similar state. As he tells us,

> An incessant stream of fantasies had been released, and I did my best not to lose my head but to find some way to understand these strange things. I stood helpless before an alien world; everything in it seemed difficult and incomprehensible. I was living in a constant state of tension; often I felt as if gigantic blocks of stone were tumbling down upon me.
>
> (Jung, 1961, p. 176)

But let's go back to Nabokov's story.

To try to find a solution to his torment, the protagonist sets off. He wants, needs, must reach his destination, but is not sure he will succeed.

> I reflected while I walked that you would probably not come to the rendez-vous. And that, if you did, we would quarrel again anyway. I only knew how to sculpt and how to love. This was not enough.

This is how we often feel when we begin an analytical journey: the paradoxical feeling of striving toward a goal despite feeling helpless, fearful and unable to reach it. It is a time of waiting or "attending" in its deepest etymological sense, which comes from the Latin *ad-tendere*, and that evokes the dynamic sense of *tend-ad* or "tend to".

The protagonist and the narrative develops around this sense of need and helplessness. The man reaches the meeting place, the Brandenburg Gate, and starts to wait, to "attend". Around him, the movement of the people, of employees returning home, of buses on their routes is a counterpoint to the cold shadow in the corner where he waits, between the columns, near the grated window of a guard post.

And here, while anxiously searching for his beloved, the man notices something, or rather, someone.

> On a stool sat a brown little old woman, short legged, plump, with a round, speckled face and she too was waiting.

The new character entering the story is unexpected, unknown and seemingly insignificant. The protagonist pays attention only because he finds her nearby. There is a stand selling postcards, maps, fans and color photos and the old woman is the seller. There is no apparent connection between the sculptor in love and this elderly woman, whose expression seems to say:

> I just happen to be here [. . .]. I sat down for a minute [. . .]. Yes, there's some kind of stand nearby, with excellent, curious knickknacks . . . But I have nothing to do with it.

However, she "attended" as well. And now the protagonist marvels at the meaning of this image, which stands out against the others, in the randomness of the comings and goings that afternoon: by virtue of a random connection, two different people of different age, social status, culture and appearance are united by their existential situation. Both are awaiting someone. And our protagonist comes to ask himself a question, for the first time not only regarding his own fate, but also that of another person:

> I wondered which of us would wait longer, and who would come first, a customer or you?

The visual horizon is widening. It has been enough to look around, to notice the seemingly insignificant movement of things. And something has happened. Or someone has come. In this case, a *companion in misfortune*. A person in the same condition, able to catch the involuntary sympathy of our protagonist. Of course, the mere appearance of a similarity of condition is not enough to change the course of the man's life or his state of mind. He continues to suffer, waiting. But now, his expectation is no longer the same, because a representation of images is arising inside him, whose therapeutic and transformative power is due, as C.G. Jung explains, to the adoption of the "attitude" of active imagination:

> To the extent that I managed to translate the emotions into images – that is to say, to find the images which were concealed in the emotions – I was inwardly calmed and reassured. [. . .] As a result of my experiment I learned how helpful it can be, from the therapeutic point of view, to find the particular images which lie behind emotions [. . .] For as long as we do not understand their meaning, such fantasies are a diabolical mixture of the sublime and the ridiculous
>
> (Jung, 1961, p. 220)

In fact, now also for Nabokov's sculptor, vision and outlook have been split into two parts, isolating the image from the emotions it possessed. . ., making him feel (like Jung), in the grip of a diabolical mixture of the sublime and the ridiculous such as to cause him to burst into laughter without knowing why:

> I started laughing, and had no idea why; perhaps it was simply because I had spent the entire night sitting in a wicker armchair, surrounded by rubbish and shards of plaster Paris, amid the dust of congealed plasticine, thinking of you.

Our man is no longer waiting only for himself but also for the old lady from the stand. His affective energy is no longer exclusively catalyzed by a *woman-Anima* which possesses him, but also by another human being. And this shift in the field, this possible adoption of a different *attitude* (the one active imagination makes possible, as Adler would explain), allows him to experience *curiosity*, the spring, the spark, which can ignite a blaze of light and warmth in the cold of depression and pain. This is the narrative expedient that gives the story its bite, that makes us want *to move on* to find out *what will happen next, how it will end*. From time immemorial, it is thanks to this existential curiosity about the unknown and new, manifested through the *animation* and *activation of the images* (and therefore of storytelling) that we can . . . save our lives, as Scheherazade teaches us with her storytelling. Scheherazade who can survive just because she is able to keep the king in a state of doubt about what is going to happen next, stopping in mid-sentence, and leaving him in a state of suspense and curiosity; "At this moment Sharazade saw the morning appearing and, discreet, was silent." (Forster, 1927)

As E.M. Forster noticed, this little phrase, seemingly without interest, is the backbone of the *Arabian Nights*, and is the creative gimmick through which the life of a very resourceful princess is spared.

Here, with this unexpected spark of curiosity and this widening of his point of view, things change for the protagonist of our story. He has now been waiting for an hour, it is getting colder and colder, the woman he awaits has not yet arrived and he is still suffering. But now his suffering has become *empathic*. It is no longer only a *self-referential* pain. No one has approached either him or the old vendor. He is able to put himself in her shoes and imagine and feel what she feels:

> My guess is she was conjuring up a rich foreigner from the Adlon Hotel who would buy all her wares, and overpay, and order more, many more picture post-cards and guidebooks of all kinds. And she probably was not very warm either in that velour jacket.

Just like in every fairy tale, being able to enter into a new situation, unknown and different, sacrificing *something of ourselves in favor of another or others,* makes us able to work that magic that C.G. Jung called *transformation.* And it is exactly at this point that something happens:

> Suddenly the window of the guardhouse opened, and a green soldier hailed the old woman. She quickly scrambled down from her stool and, with her thrust-out-belly, scuttled up to the window. With a relaxed motion, the soldier handed her a streaming mug and closed the sash. His green shoulder turned and with-drew into the murky depths.

What happens in the story, this unexpected, let's call it *twist*, does not happen to the protagonist, but to the old vendor. But, by virtue of the *transformation* generated by the widening of his horizon and empathic understanding, the positive occurrence for the woman is reflected in the man, and marks a significant turning point for him. Now he observes and *understands* the feelings and the life of another human being. A shivering woman drinking a hot cup of coffee is no longer insignificant to him, plagued as he is by the penalty of love . . . because he is now able to feel empathy not only for the suffering, but also for the *pleasure* of others:

> She drank for a long time, drank in slow swallows, reverently licking off the fringe of skin, heating her palms on the warm tin. And a dark, sweet warmth poured into my soul. My soul too, was drinking and heating itself, and the brown little woman tasted of coffee with milk.

The possibility of time-off from our own pain. The chance to look around. The opportunity to discover there is an affinity and a connection between our lives, our suffering and our joy, and the lives, suffering and joy of others, dispels the *invisibility of the obvious* (Collura, 2004), and it allows for another way of seeing and feeling the world. The point of view of the narrative and the experience is then overturned. All that Nabokov can tell us through the perception of the sculptor

And at that instant you arrived, at last, or, rather not you, but a German couple.

Now that the wait of the sculptor has become the wait of the little old brown woman, the hope is that the two Germans will buy something. They linger, look, consider . . . but do not buy. The couple leaves without buying anything. But the sculptor can experience this frustration in a different way. Like the old brown woman who

> Only smiled, replaced her postcards in their slots, and again became absorbed in her red book.

You may suffer a loss, pain and lack . . . but if you are passionate about something and you are not only acting to fulfill your needs, loss and pain become tolerable. For the old brown lady, the pleasure of reading her "red book" (synchronic coincidence . . . with the remarks I am making!) and the unexpected gift of a glass of warm milk and coffee, make life valuable and satisfying even though it is materially disadvantaged and (apparently) without success. The soul of our sculptor is imbued with this new way of experiencing life . . . and is moved.

So far I presented the story of Nabokov. But what about us? As analytical psychologists that refer to Jung's concept, what is our role in this transformation? How can we help to facilitate it and activate it through our work?

As Jung reminds us:

> The *causa efficiens* of the transubstantiation is a spontaneous act of God's grace. [. . .]. In the ritual action man places himself at the disposal of an autonomous and "eternal" agency operating outside the categories of human consciousness – *si parva licet componere magnis* – in much the same way that a good actor does not merely represent the drama, but allows himself to be overpowered by the genius of the dramatist.
>
> (Jung, 1941, par. 379)

That is to say, we must be able to activate the "attitude" of active imagination in our patients, enabling them to be possessed by the genius of the playwright, not so much rationally teaching them to "see" and "understand" psychic images materialized in their unconscious, but accompanying them in the enterprise of experiencing the deepest symbolic meaning, both individually and collectively, in the everyday world. But we will never be able to do this if we have not lived through the same experience. Active imagination indeed is not something you can teach or explain, but "only" embody existentially. To use Nabokov's metaphor, not only must we somehow acquire that special ability to tell a seemingly trivial story, revealing, layer by layer, the different levels of meaning; we should also have lived through it, and therefore be able to empathically share the painful anguish of the sculptor. We should also possess, embody and represent the Calvinian lightness, that "special lyrical and existential modulation which allows us to contemplate our own drama as if from outside and to dissolve it with melancholy and irony" (Calvino, 1993, pp. 24–25). Like Nabokov's old lady who is able to receive and enjoy the gift of charity, just because she knows how to live patiently and lightly.

I believe this means putting ourselves at the disposal of that autonomous "Eternal" or "Operator" that exists beyond the categories of consciousness. And for this reason, alone and with our patients, we could experience what Jung called our "Being there, no longer alone, out of time, belonging to the centuries" (Jung, 1944, par. 177).

And like the sculptor of our story, having access to a truly significant and profound transformation that Vladimir Nabokov describes as follows:

> Here I became aware of the world's tenderness, the profound beneficence of all that surrounded me, the blissful bond between me and all of creation, and I realized that the joy I sought in you was not only secreted within you, but breathed around me everywhere, in the speeding street sounds, in the hem of a comically lifted skirt, in the metallic yet tender drone of the wind, in the autumn clouds bloated with rain. I realized that the world does not represent a struggle at all, or a predaceous sequence of chance events, but the shimmering bliss, beneficent trepidation, a gift bestowed upon us and unappreciated.

Notes

1 This chapter was originally a paper presented at the Fourth Joint Conference of the IAAP and IAJS: "Psyche, Spirit, and Science: Negotiating Contemporary Social and Cultural Concerns", July 9–12, 2015, Yale University, New Haven, USA.
2 In the Italian version, the title of the story *Beneficence* was translated in the collection of short stories, "La Veneziana", Adelphi 1992, with the title "La grazia".

References

Adler, G. (1966). *Studies in Analytical Psychology*. London: Hodder and Stoughton.
Calvino, I. (1993). "La leggerezza". In: *Lezioni americane*. Milan: Mondadori.
Collura, M. (2004). *In Sicilia*. Milan: Longanesi.
Forster, E.M. (1927). *Aspects of the Novel*. New York: Harcourt, Brace.
Jung, C.G. (1935). *The Tavistock Lectures, On the Theory and Practice of Analytical Psychology*. In: *Collected Works*, vol. 18, London: Routledge and Kegan Paul.
Jung, C.G. (1941). *Transformation Symbolism in the Mass*, par. 379. In: *Collected Works*, vol. 11. London: Routledge & Kegan Paul.
Jung, C.G. (1944). *Psychology and Alchemy*, par. 177. In: *Collected Works*, vol. 12. London: Routledge & Kegan Paul.
Jung, C.G. (1946–47). *On the Nature of the Psyche*, par. 400. In: *Collected Works*, vol. 8. London: Routledge & Kegan Paul.
Jung, C.G. (1957). *The Transcendent Function*, par. 134. In: *Collected Works*, vol. 8. London: Routledge & Kegan Paul.
Jung, C.G. (1961). *Memories, Dreams, Reflections by C.G. Jung*, recorded and edited by Aniela Jaffé, p. 176. New York: Vintage Books.
Jung, C.G. (2009). *The Red Book*, edited by Sonu Shamdasani, pp. 273, 27/28. New York and London: Norton.
Nabokov, V. (1924). *Beneficence*. In: Nabokov D. et al., eds., *The Stories of Vladimir Nabokov*. New York: Knopf, 1995.
Nabokov, V. (1966). *Speak, Memory*. New York: Putmans Sons.
Nabokov, V. (1973). *Strong Opinion*. New York: McGraw-Hill.

Chapter 8

Imaginations

Dario Voltolini

It is always useful for those who produce artistic artifacts to think about the concept of "imagination". It is an intuitive concept, but as soon as you have a closer look, it becomes very hard to define, which is why I will not try to do so.

Imagination is a human faculty that allows us to somehow recall nonexistent things, events that did not happen, interpretations that differ from a given reality. This is not meant to be a definition, but rather a reminder of what we normally mean when we use this word in our everyday life. If it were a definition, it would be wrong in many ways – especially the term "given reality", which seems to have a meaning but maybe does not.[1]

If we take the term "imagination" in its intuitive meaning in common language, it is clear we resort to it constantly in our life.

Narrowing it down to artistic activity, we are able to say something that is not meaningless. Further narrowing it down to my form of art, that is, writing, and to that of the writers I read and who help me through their works to better understand what I do, or what I would like to do, or what I see possible, I will say a few things.

I will say them by using the phases of what Jung called "Active Imagination" as my guide.[2]

Active Imagination is a tool, a practice used in the therapeutic relationship between the analyst and the patient. As such, it does not necessarily have anything to do with producing something artistic. In the therapeutic process triggered by Active Imagination, the patient is able to confront their own visions that emerge from the unconscious and are presented to them as objects and interlocutors.

In the making of art, it is clear the same thing happens.[3] The same but also different. The same thing happens because, also in the making of art, contents emerge – we may say substantially from nothingness or emptiness; contents that will eventually be brought into the world we are all part of by an artistic process. Assuming that these contents arise (or seem to arise) from nothingness and emptiness, this first part of art-making is essentially the same as the first phase of Active Imagination described as "emptying", "letting things happen".

This is where, I believe, things immediately become complicated. If I think about the books I wrote, I must recognize that each one was born from a condition

DOI: 10.4324/9781003411383-8

of "emptiness". At a certain point in my life, out of nowhere, the seed of what I would write came to life. But I must also recognize it was different for each book. The way books come to life can be different each time: I imagined my first book as a series of pictures to be described;[4] the second as the duty to bear witness to facts from the workplace I shared with others, and which only I could recount (I worked in an IT company with colleagues from different backgrounds, mainly technical and scientific – I was the only writer so it was up to me to recount what was happening[5]); I imagined the third as the literary transposition of an acoustic fact into stories; that is, the difference in the timbre when playing the same note with different instruments, the difference between sounds of the same frequency, but with different waveforms; I imagined the fourth as a result of a commission of a newspaper that had asked me to write ten stories on soccer, giving me "freedom to imagine them" as I saw fit.[6] And so on.

In my creative experience, "emptiness" and "letting things happen" are really difficult moments to bring back to a basic unity. But there is no doubt there is a moment, very mysterious yet very common in my opinion, when something that did not exist starts to exist. As for my personal experience, I will share a memory with you.

I remember very well that I was working doggedly on creating, in my imagination, a long text. I was thinking and rethinking the structure. I was trying to imagine (very actively!) the scenes I would describe, the sequence of facts I wanted to tell. I was trying to imagine its ending, the point at which the whole narrative was to converge and which would give me the idea to write the passages leading to that ending. I had loads of notes, written on pieces of paper chaotically placed in a box. Yet, despite my best efforts, I could not do it; I could not "see" it, I could not imagine it, I could not start to write. Every time I was about to face the issue, something else would come to my mind, something that had nothing to do with what I wanted to write. At some point, I decided to write down the other things coming to my mind to get them out of the way, to get rid of them as if they were (they actually were) obstacles to what I wanted to do. And so I wrote the storybook based on the differences in sound waves.[7]

Where did they come from? All my imagination, all my fantasy driven by desire and consciousness, was focused on the long text I wanted to write. That imagination was, or rather seemed, very active. Instead, somewhere else, out of nowhere, those stories were coming to me. When I further looked into what Jung said about Active Imagination, I then realized that my first imagination was guided by consciousness, while what appeared later, seemingly out of nowhere, came from the unconscious; just like what happens to those who, thanks to *emptying*, are able to bring out seemingly foreign content, precisely because they are unconscious.

This memory makes me think that, perhaps, imagination has more ramifications than we think. Specifically, at that stage of my work, I clearly had two imaginations: one congested and apparently hyperactive, although blocked, and the other apparently nonexistent, unconscious, and yet it allowed me to write a book. Not the book I was working on (and which I eventually wrote later, after clearing the field of the voices that were distracting me from it[8]), but another one, completely unexpected.

I would like to continue talking about the possibility that imagination is an articulate, plural faculty, full of aspects that perhaps have nothing in common, or maybe they do.

Apart from finding this plurality in my personal creative experience, I find it in that of the other authors I am lucky enough to work with in person, and of course in many of the authors of the endless literary and, more generally, artistic corpus we have at our disposal (our only time machine, for now).

I will give a few examples, which I think may be useful in relation to the second phase of Active Imagination as Jungian analysis sees it: that of accepting the irrational and incomprehensible.

I cannot say I have experience in accepting irrational or incomprehensible objects, situations or visions into my writing-related imagination. But I do have experience in dealing with and wanting to accept the unpredictable. I created a text whose structure was up to chance and not up to me. Similar to what happens in certain musical compositions (Cage, Xenakis, Eno, etc.),[9] I had entrusted part of the drafting of the book to chance. I gave myself a period of time; whatever text I was commissioned to write in that time, I would write as a chapter of the book.[10] Therefore, before the time was up, I had no way of knowing – and I never knew – how many chapters would make up my book. It was a game, of course. But in that time my imagination was open and willing to welcome inputs from others, inputs that went beyond me.

I also had the experience of an image coming back to me and whose origin I did not understand. The image kept coming back to me, outside of my work as a writer. I confronted it and processed it into writing much later. It was the image of a rather wide paving stone being submerged by sea waves. The waves were rushing over the stones and then flowing away. The scene appeared to me as a place I had seen in the past, and it carried along a very strong emotional component. I now know that Jung was also unexpectedly "assaulted" by the appearance of real and symbolic waves in his life.[11] Working on it led to discovering it was a hybrid between the cathedral in Trani, Piazza Unità d'Italia in Trieste, and a verse by Keats:[12] ". . . magic casements, opening on the foam/Of perilous seas, in faery lands forlorn".[13]

I do not know how, where, when and why these three elements had mixed.

Speaking of accepting in imagination, I would like to present someone else's experience and the work of a poet.

The experience is that of writer Antonio Moresco, an author of the utmost importance in contemporary literature. His main work consists of the trilogy "Games of Eternity",[14] an extraordinarily complex and visionary work, several thousand pages long. Moresco says the whole work suddenly flashed into his mind, like lightning, while he was in Calabria years ago. Taking it in meant years and years of writing. And now it exists for all of us.[15]

The work of the poet is "The Changing Light at Sandover",[16] written by James Merrill. In composing the poem, Merrill incorporated occult messages from the afterlife which came from the mediumship use of a Ouija board. It is an extremely important work of literature, 560 pages long. Speaking of the dead and the afterlife, there is something amusing and ironic in the fact that Jung, in *The Red Book*, quotes this phrase of the Serpent/Soul: "I believe the dead will soon become extinct."[17] In Italian we use the expression "i cari estinti", "the dearly extinct", to refer to dead family members. If even the dead are becoming extinct, does that mean our loved ones are becoming even more extinct in the realm of the dead? This is not only an amusing curiosity but a specter of fantasy about the different worlds: if we use the word "extinct" to refer to a person who has passed on from the world of the living to the world of the dead, where will that person pass on to if they also become extinct in the world of the dead? Is there a world of the ultra-dead where the person ends up becoming extinct in the realm of the dead? After making this assumption, it is easy to see the possibility of regression to infinity (do they end up in the realm of ultra-ultra-death? And from this into the realm of ultra-ultra-ultra-mortality and so on in an infinite regression of extinctions?) Or, by also becoming extinct in the realm of death, does the person go into nothingness and the story just ends there? Or do they become extinct in the realm of death to return to that of life, in an eternal coming and going? (Antonio Moresco puts this idea into the structure of hard-boiled detective fiction, with a very interesting outcome.[18]) Or is there a series of realms to pass into, but instead of regressing to infinity, they form a chain that after, who knows how many and above all which stops, takes us back to the "starting point", to the so-called world of the living, that is, our own world? What if the chain is not sequential, but rather a matrix, a chessboard? What if the matrix were three-dimensional? And, at this point, what if it were multidimensional? And so on? Oh, Carl Gustav, what a joke you made in that book of yours! Look at all that you triggered in just one line!

Regarding the relationship with the dead, we should also mention the beautiful "Here Is Where We Meet", by writer, draftsman and art critic, John Berger: it is meaningful that such a book came from the pen of an avowed historical materialist.[19]

These few examples alone clearly show that there is not only one way of accepting in imagination, but, once again, there are several ways.[20]

Regarding the third phase of Active Imagination – that of the representation of the content that emerged – the activity of the patient with the analyst and that of the artwork creator do not exactly match, in my opinion. Regarding artistic activity, the work, and in principle the production of objects that can be used by others, there are very specific and sectoral factors related to the structure and the history of one's art; choices are made in terms of poetics and relationship with other authors, whether contemporary or from the past, and in terms of intention for the shape the artistic object will have.

Allow me to say a few things about the representation of content. Actually, I would like to say four things.

Here comes the first. For the artistic form of writing (but not only that one), choosing the so-called "point of view" is normal, yet essential. This is another imprecise concept, but we can all agree on its meaning. When a writer sets their work, they must – whether they like it or not – choose a point of view. Usually more than one, indeed: their point of view as author, the point of view of the narrator, the points of view of the characters. Furthermore, the points of view, which can change throughout the same work, can even enter into a complex relationship with one another.[21] Just to give you an example, in a beautiful storybook by Marta Cai, *Enti di ragione*,[22] Character A in Story S, for example, told from Character B's point of view, is present in Story S's as a narrator with his/her own point of view. The stories reflect one another and push the reader to different and interesting reinterpretations, due to retroactive games that intertwine all the stories. After watching the world from Character A's point of view, the story where he/she is narrated from a different point of view acquires new meanings, and so on. This is to say that the point of view can become a narrative item, contributing to the development of the final object.

However, we should say that, as highlighted by Tozzi,[23] even the process of Active Imagination may include the "imaginative" point of view, thanks to the possibility of shifting energy from the Ego to the unconscious, and therefore from a subjective point of view to a more objective point of view, which can be identified in the different figures/characters emerging from the unconscious.

This seems to be linked to the quivers of living your life even if it really isn't your life. A work staging and presenting such a scenario enriches the reader and their imagination. An example of successful work in this regard is the book *L'esercizio*,[24] by Claudia Petrucci. Here, the game is sophisticated: there is a girl and, when she plays as a theater actress, she identifies with the character she interprets to the point that she becomes that character even in real life. When this process becomes clinical, her boyfriend and her director imagine a "real and ordinary life" for her, in order to treat her. They treat her by leveraging her own disease. So, by following this tailor-made script, the girl will live a life which is twice as much not her own.

The second thing I would like to say is not related to writing, but to the work of artist Corrado Ambrogio. Over the years, his artistic production has refined the so-called "object trouvé" poetics with much elegance and cheerful irony. I'm mentioning this here because Corrado Ambrogio's talent in naming an object was outstanding. A wooden log, found in the woods, called "spider" and exhibited to the public, would forever remain a spider in the memory of those who saw it. A number of metal hooks for harvesting bought throughout years of rural fairs, geometrically arranged in an installation, were given the name "the army", and for the visitors that would forever be their name. The artistic talent of naming is to me an important element of artistic imagination and the same is true for writing, of course. Corrado Ambrogio's example shows there is another function of imagination that comes into play in art; that is, naming content that has not emerged but has been found, that becomes something else precisely after the act of naming.[25]

Please allow me a quick digression here. The form of art I'm talking about is essentially writing, since this is my area of expertise. But there is another reason why writing, as well as dance[26] and, partially, singing, make sense in relation to the form of imagination I believe Jung was referring to. And such reason is that writing – as well as dance – uses language as a means of expression (dance uses the body) which is a uniquely human object.[27] Language exists because so does humankind. If we were to disappear, colors and marble would remain, even sounds would remain, but language would not (neither would our bodies, by definition). On this topic, see the essayistic activity of the linguist and writer Andrea Moro, in particular his "I Speak, Therefore I Am".[28] I would like to end this quick digression with the following remark: if the fact that shared archetypes live deep down is a discovery, then the fact that words, syntax and semantics are the same for everybody is mere and trivial evidence. It lies on a rock.

My third thought has to do with a little book by Gherardo Bortolotti, *Tutte le camere d'albergo del mondo*,[29] in which the author addresses the novel narration from a point of view that we could label as anti-novel, producing an extremely interesting, short-circuited text where each chapter is the description of an imagined novel which could be written, but is not. The sequence of these chapters – kept together by the precise and fine narrative move of the last chapter – results in a narration made of novels that are imagined but not produced. I believe this precious literary contribution is a useful and relevant example of Active Imagination applied to other *n* imaginations which remain undeveloped. The short-circuit lies here: the author's meta-imagination is in action, resulting in a sequence of possible and not current narrations. In my opinion, imagining other imaginations is very interesting for what we are focusing on.

The fourth thing has to do with the work of writer Giulio Mozzi, namely his *Le ripetizioni*.[30] At the heart of his literary production there is a fierce meditation on the Evil. In *Le ripetizioni*, the character presents with such perfect cruelty it cannot be invoked here; you need to enter the pages and meet him. Mozzi said he has a monster inside and he is dealing with it. The dynamics here are very interesting, especially because they are in the work of a writer who, even from a theological perspective, asks fundamental questions about the concept of salvation. His meditation on the Evil is as important as his literary outcome. Facing the monster is linked to therapeutic Active Imagination, both in the phase of accepting the irrational and in the phase of its representation. Here, with Mozzi, literary imagination gets closer to therapeutic imagination, at least in some respects. This allows us to move directly to the phase of ethical comparison of Active Imagination, where perhaps all the threads of imaginations, that started together and then drifted apart, converge.

How to deal with the plural form "imaginations"? I believe we need to move towards the very concept of imagination. Not only to clearly outline its borders and essence, but rather to try a kind of controversial game; that is, trying to imagine what we would like imagination to be. I believe that even this slightly elusive faculty we have can evolve. And maybe we should start to imagine in which direction we want it to evolve. I said something provisional on this topic – and I even said it quite poorly – during a TEDx conference.[31]

Let me summarize it and conclude. I imagine an imagination that increasingly develops its ability to match things (in the sense of the "symbol") without forgetting its ability to separate from the factual datum; I imagine an imagination that is able to always find the unique root of its own creations, increasingly different from one another, meaning that while producing new things, it is able to always go back to what brings together, for example, smartphones and the Fosbury flop; I imagine an imagination that does not lose connection with the linear flow of time, but that most of all feels increasingly comfortable in the non-linear time that is not only in our depths, but right in reality, and whose nature is also revealing, as Jung already knew very well, in the scientific field.

But this last thing is something writers have always known.

Notes

1 As an example, among many others, see Nelson Goodman ("Ways of Worldmaking", Hackett, 1978) and how reality as we perceive it is the result of our construction and imagination work.

2 For the concept of "Active Imagination", see Joan Chodorow, "Jung on Active Imagination", Princeton University Press, 1997.

3 Tozzi, C. (2014) "En Route: from Active Imagination to Film Language" in *Proceedings of the 19th Congress of the International Association for Analytical Psychology*, Daimon Verlag.

4 Voltolini, D. (1990) *Una intuizione metropolitana*, Bollati Boringhieri.

5 Voltolini, D. (1994) *Rincorse*, Einaudi.

6 Voltolini, D. (2018) *10*, Feltrinelli, 2000. Laurana (ebook).

7 Voltolini, D. (2013) *Forme d'onda*, Feltrinelli, 1996. Laurana (ebook).

8 Voltolini, D. (2001) *Primaverile (uomini nudi al testo)*, Feltrinelli.

9 Very relevant in this regard is the music experiment "INTRO-SPETTRO" by Giacomo Aiolli where chance, synchronicity, choice, cause and effect relationship are managed by a stochastic algorithm to produce the artistic-musical outcome. I think the mysterious fascination at the very core of the idea that an algorithm is stochastic has much to say about the profound meaning of "imagination".

10 Voltolini, D. (2015) *Autunnale (dalla finestra sul teatro)*, BookSprint Edizioni.

11 Tozzi, C. (2020) "Affrontare le onde", *Studi Junghiani*, vol. 26, n. 2.

12 Keats, J. (1977) "Ode to a Nightingale", in *John Keats, The Complete Poems*, Penguin Classics.

13 I talk about this here: https://www.nazioneindiana.com/2004/09/27/lavori-in-corso/.

14 For the only review of the entire work, as far as I know, see: https://theuntranslated. wordpress.com/2018/07/31/games-of-eternity-giochi-delleternita-by-antonio-moresco/.

15 I talk about Moresco here: "Riflessioni di un accanito lettore", in: *Uno scrittore visionario. Antonio Moresco*, Effigie, 2019.

16 Merrill, J. (2006) "The Changing Light at Sandover" (1982), 14th ed. Knopf.

17 Jung, C.G. (2016) *Das Rote Buch*, Patmos Verlag, 175/176 (in the Italian edition, Bollati Boringhieri, 2010, p. 323).

18 Moresco, A. (2019) "Canto di D'Arco", SEM.

19 Berger, J. (2006) *Here Is Where We Meet: A Story of Crossing Paths*, Vintage.

20 The connection between imagination, invention and discovery in relation to Nikola Tesla is very interesting. I talk about it here: https://www.leparoleelecose.it/?p=37156.

21 For the point of view linked to Active Imagination, see: Tozzi, C. (2015) "Reason and Wrong: Analytical Psychology, Fiction and Analytical Stance. A Confrontation", in *IAAP, International Association for Analytical Psychology. The Analyst in The Polis. Volume I. Proceedings from the Second Conference on Analysis and Activism: Social and Political Contributions of Jungian Psychology*, Rome; Tozzi, C. (2017) "Il viaggio del paziente sceneggiatore: dall'immaginazione attiva al linguaggio di un film", *Rivista di Psicologia Analitica*, n. 44, Astrolabio Ed, vol. 96/2017; Tozzi, C. (2007) *Il paziente sceneggiatore. Raccontare storie in analisi e in un film*, Gaffi Editore, 2007; Tozzi, C. (2017) "A Different Way of Being in the World: The Attitude of the Patient Scriptwriter", *Journal of Analytical Psychology*, n. 62(2), April 2017; Tozzi, C. (2017) "A Different Way of Being in the World" in *Proceedings of the 20th Congress of the International Association for Analytical Psychology*, Daimon Verlag Ed.
22 Cai, M. (2019) "Enti di ragione", Sui Generis. I. In: *DoppioZero*. https://www.doppiozero.com/le-nostre-solitudini.
23 See Tozzi, C., "The Experience of Grace: The Possibility of Transformation in Vladimir Nabokov and Carl Gustav Jung" (Chapter 7 of this volume).
24 Petrucci, C. (2020) *L'esercizio*, La nave di Teseo.
25 My tribute to Corrado Ambrogio: https://www.doppiozero.com/corrado-ambrogio-il-malinconico-ilare-genio-gentile.
26 Tozzi, C., "A Rite of Passage, Interview with Elsa Piperno" (Chapter 5 of this volume).
27 Fleisher, K., "The Origin and History of Embodied Active Imagination: Authentic Movement Through the Life and Work of Its Early Pioneers" (Chapter 2 of this volume).
28 Moro, A. (2016) *I Speak, Therefore I Am. Seventeen Thoughts About Language*, Columbia University Press.
29 Bortolotti, G. (2022) *Tutte le camere d'albergo del mondo*, Hopefulmonster editore.
30 Mozzi, G. (2021) *Le ripetizioni*, Marsilio.
31 Voltolini, D. (2021) "Immaginare una nuova immaginazione". TEDx Talks. https://youtu.be/QlSLDBosYu0.

References

Berger, J. (2006) *Here Is Where We Meet: A Story of Crossing Paths*, Vintage.
Bortolotti, G. (2022) *Tutte le camere d'albergo del mondo*, Hopefulmonster editore.
Cai, M. (2019) "Enti di ragione", Sui Generis. I. In: *DoppioZero*. https://www.doppiozero.com/le-nostre-solitudini.
Chodorow, J. (1997) *Jung on Active Imagination*, Princeton University Press.
Goodman, N. (1978) *Ways of Worldmaking*, Hackett.
Jung, C.G. (2016) *Das Rote Buch*, Patmos Verlag, 175/176 (in the Italian edition, Bollati Boringhieri, 2010, p. 323).
Keats, J. (1977) "Ode to a Nightingale", in "John Keats, "The Complete Poems", Penguin Classics.
Merrill J. (2006) "The Changing Light at Sandover" (1982), 14th ed., Knopf.
Moresco, A. (2019) *Canto di D'Arco*, SEM.
Moro, A. (2016) *I Speak, Therefore I am. Seventeen Thoughts About Language*, Columbia University Press.
Mozzi, G. (2021) *Le ripetizioni*, Marsilio.
Petrucci, C. (2020) *L'esercizio*, La nave di Teseo.
Tozzi, C. (2007) *Il paziente sceneggiatore. Raccontare storie in analisi e in un film*, Gaffi Editore, 2007.

Tozzi, C. (2014) "En Route: from Active Imagination to Film Language" in *Proceedings of the 19th Congress of the International Association for Analytical Psychology*, Daimon Verlag.

Tozzi, C. (2015) "Reason and Wrong: Analytical Psychology, Fiction and Analytical Stance. A Confrontation", in *IAAP, International Association for Analytical Psychology. The Analyst in The Polis. Volume I. Proceedings from the Second Conference on Analysis and Activism: Social and Political Contributions of Jungian Psychology*, Rome.

Tozzi, C. (2017) "A Different Way of Being in the World: The Attitude of the Patient Scriptwriter", *Journal of Analytical Psychology*, 62(2), April 2017.

Tozzi, C. (2017) "A Different Way of Being in the World" in *Proceedings of the 20th Congress of the International Association for Analytical Psychology*, Daimon Verlag Ed.

Tozzi, C. (2017) "Il viaggio del paziente sceneggiatore: dall'immaginazione attiva al linguaggio di un film", *Rivista di Psicologia Analitica*, 96(44), Astrolabio Ed.

Tozzi, C. (2020) "Affrontare le onde", *Studi Junghiani*, 26(2).

Voltolini, D. (1990) *Una intuizione metropolitana*, Bollati Boringhieri.

Voltolini, D. (1994) *Rincorse*, Einaudi.

Voltolini, D. (2001) *Primaverile (uomini nudi al testo)*, Feltrinelli.

Voltolini, D. (2013) *Forme d'onda*, Feltrinelli, 1996. Laurana (ebook).

Voltolini, D. (2015) "Autunnale (dalla finestra sul teatro)", BookSprint Edizioni.

Voltolini, D. (2018) *10*, Feltrinelli, 2000. Laurana, (ebook).

Voltolini, D. (2019) "Riflessioni di un accanito lettore", in: *Uno scrittore visionario*. Antonio Moresco, Effigie.

Voltolini, D. (2021) "Immaginare una nuova immaginazione". TEDx Talks. https://youtu.be/QlSLDBosYu0.

Chapter 9

Impalpable and Shooting for the Clouds

Interview with Umberto Contarello

Chiara Tozzi

This interview was carried out in February 2022, at dinner time. Umberto asked me if he could invite Edoardo and Filippo – two young assistants who graduated in Screenwriting at the Centro Sperimentale di Cinematografia in Rome – to take part, just as in the best tradition of the history of Italian screenwriting, perfecting their craft "in the workshop".

Following Umberto's recommendations, during the interview Edoardo and Filippo were cooking pasta. I intentionally chose not to cut out the parts where Umberto talks to the two young assistants because I believe Active Imagination, the ideation and creation of a story, and the art of cooking in some way relate to one another, taking us back to the alchemical transformation which, for Jung, is a metaphor for the psychological process that aims to give shape to the imaginary attitudes of every human being.

Tozzi *Umberto, do you know anything about C.G. Jung's Active Imagination?*

Contarello *Very little, and it's for the best.*

Tozzi *I agree. I want to start by saying that Active Imagination is a method first experimented by Jung on himself, which he then defined as the elective method to face the unconscious, both within a therapeutic process, i.e. with the analyst, and independently. Today, I would like to explore the possible correlation between the phases of Active Imagination and the expression of the psyche in creating a story, especially considering your role as screenwriter, and therefore in the design and creation of a story for a film. I will present to you the four phases of Active Imagination and, phase by phase, you can tell me if there are any similarities to your way of working and coming up with an idea for a film and then the actual writing of the film.*

Contarello Perfect.

Contarello [to Edoardo and Filippo] Guys, did you hear that? Are you there?

Edoardo and Filippo Yes, we're here. All clear!

Contarello [to Edoardo and Filippo] Ok, listen to me: there is a big pot on the last shelf on the left. Fill it up with water and start cooking the pasta.

Contarello Ok, we can start!

DOI: 10.4324/9781003411383-9

Tozzi *The first phase of Active Imagination can be defined as letting things happen, emptying the mind that Jung describes as doing by not doing; a receptive abandonment, a willingness to be open to images with no interferences of the consciousness. Are there any similarities to your way of abandoning yourself to the ideas and images that lead you to creating a story for a film?*

Contarello   In my way of working, this is not fundamental; but it was an achievement. An achievement I reached after spending the evening with Fabrizio de André[1] after what, sadly, was his last concert at Teatro Brancaccio in Rome. That evening he told me something crucial. I had asked him if he took notes of the things he considered meaningful before writing a song. He answered that, at first, he did, but then he stopped because he realized memory is like a fishing net abandoned at sea, and fish get caught in it. When you start writing, the fish jump up from the water – what you will truly need is what gets caught in the net. I also think that what you can use and what is useful gets caught in your memory's fishing net and reappears when you need it. Fantasy at work attracts the fish that come to the surface. It has to do with synchronicity: the hint for a narration doesn't arise like a need – needs are physical, they have nothing to do with this – but only at the right time. It appears all of a sudden, like an epiphany. I test this epiphany with duration. It appears, and I just stay there to watch and see if it's a comet or a star. The star doesn't move, but when I start writing, I do so in synchronicity with the fish that jumped out of need, that appeared. Duration and synchronicity are not diametrically opposed. After that evening with Fabrizio De André I found the courage to never take notes again; I trusted the duration. Duration is the measure of what resonates within. What doesn't resonate within does not, it goes away. In some way, we are dealing with a sort of storage, so to speak, a big fish tank where to pick from – or actually, where we unconsciously pick from when our thoughts need those goldfish or that furniture kept in storage. This is duration. It means persistence. This part of creating a story requires the unconscious, abandonment, and the non-decision between what is important and what isn't, because you only realize something is important later on, not while it is happening.

Tozzi *You are saying that during the creative process that then leads to putting an idea into focus, it has become and is easy for you to abandon yourself and have faith without doing?*

Contarello   Yes. I think the most important part of my work is when I am not working. We all interpret our work based on our personality. As an orphan, I have always lived a sort of self-made life and I therefore never did anything with clarity. I wandered. At some point I realized the only thing I needed to write was what was caught in the net.

Tozzi *Are you patient and do you have faith?*

Contarello   This is a good question. I have a presumptuous faith and patience, meaning that I have become presumptuous that I don't need to do what others do.

Let's say I've reached the last stage of a presumptuous person, as I am one of them. And also: I presume I will not miss anything good and important.

Tozzi   *Does this presumption that you won't miss anything good and important come from something that exists between you and the good and important thing? Is there a third element or is it just something about yourself?*

Contarello   Well, I have to admit something terrible: the truth, the only serious thing about Narcissus is that he establishes everything. Having married and having died for himself, the whole memory of the couple who died – because one of the two died – is sacred and beautiful. I do not fear a bad memory, because I am Narcissus.

Tozzi   *Are you reconciled with the image of Narcissus? Do you like it? Is it something you get along with or do you suffer because of it?*

Contarello   Well, if by Narcissus we don't mean the nonsense for which some say, "He combed his hair in front of the mirror, he is so like Narcissus," rather someone who died trying to hug himself, then I am solid. In the common vision the image of Narcissus is linked to someone weak, empty. But I must say that a "serious" Narcissus is someone who goes to see his image in the lake and, seeing such a beautiful image, decides to jump in. This is Narcissus. Choppy Narcissus is the one who ruins women's lives, the one who isn't happy with the image he saw in the lake because it was a bit windy that day, so he had to go back the following day (meaning he goes back to that same woman) looking for a confirmation of that exact vision. These people are dangerous, very dangerous, because they come back looking for confirmation.

Tozzi   *And they are surely not attracted to the necessary fish.*

Contarello   Of course. They're afraid of not seeing themselves.

Tozzi   *The fear of not seeing themselves doesn't allow them to see the beautiful and necessary fish, the ones that are jumping up from the net.*

Contarello   Exactly, it is a vision without others, therefore not a vision that leads one to jump in to hug himself. If you are brave, you see clearly and you decide to marry yourself, you will also hug yourself. Dying while trying to hug yourself is like a wedding that has something gloomy with yourself. This means that in creativity . . . no, wait, I don't like this word! In fantasy, you could never think your creative idea is ugly. In fantasy, you don't care about other people's judgment because what matters is what you think of your idea. Therefore, if you are Narcissus, your idea must be a good one.

Tozzi   *We can move on to the second phase of Active Imagination when, according to Jung, you start to also consciously accept the irrational and incomprehensible. At this point, the images examined by the consciousness start to become real, they come to life, they change. How can this relate to the moment you meet those images? Do you allow the images to take a life of their own?*

Contarello   This is a question for the end of the 1800s. What I mean is that the 1800s and the beginning of the 1900s were based on hope, trust or faith. Events and feelings have a causal relationship and are therefore connected by a bond that is deeply rational. This means that I suffer, I cry; I cry and I go to her house to tell her I am crying for her; she doesn't open the door so I go back home and on the following morning I decide to forget about her. But when I decide to forget about her, she comes back to me and everything seems doable. Breaking this chain which gave me the idea that the world makes sense and therefore that the story is like a Prozac was irreplaceable for me. Hold on, I need to make sure Edoardo and Filippo are alive!

Edoardo and Filippo   We're alive. We're most definitely alive!

Contarello [to Edoardo and Filippo]   Ok, good.

Contarello   As I was saying, that vision was not replaced by a causal relationship but by a relationship of assonance, resonance. The scenes and images get in touch with one another through a musical relationship, or even better: through a lyrical and not a narrative scheme. The songs or poems don't have a cause–effect relationship with the following one, rather they resonate with it. Just think of a series of bells that resonate with one another; when you play the first, the others play as well. I try to work on the resonance and not on the cause and effect. The images are not linked by "this happened so this other thing will happen" but by "this happened and emotionally and in a way I don't fully understand, this other thing will happen". I don't see the question separating two scenes as a problem but rather as an advantage, because it keeps together a more complex question and gets rid of the "why". I worked to get rid of the "why".

Tozzi   *This resonates with Active Imagination and with what happens in the work of analysis.*

Contarello   Of course!

Tozzi   *In analytical therapy, we move forward by resonance.*

Contarello   Chiara, what I just shared with you came to surface after a long analysis with Trevi[2] and Montanari.[3] In some way, I could say they directed me toward, or maybe, they ironically led me to reduce the omnipotence of the all-knowing narrator.

Tozzi   *Which is fundamental both in analysis and in narration. You must move to decentralize yourself, and allow what is being created on its own to come to life. Without expecting us, or actually allowing consciousness, the conscious ego, to be the only creator.*

Contarello   It's easy. The all-knowing narrator discovers and then speaks. This overlap between scene and thread doesn't need prior knowledge but a sort of charm, recklessness and faith.

Tozzi   *Going back to faith, which has a lot to do with charm . . .*

Contarello   Yes, faith makes it possible for the conclusion to appear and not to be preordered.

Tozzi   *In fact, the second phase of Active Imagination is that of the appearance of something that manifests itself even without having been preordered or logically planned, and therefore causes great surprise.*

Contarello   Yes, it is something that happens after you practice it. It starts to appear, you only see a part of it, and it makes you giggle; it makes you think "it could end up like this!" I think that knowing first and saying later is a deadly operation. It's just like . . . What's it called when there are dead bodies and they perform an . . .

Tozzi   *Forensic doctors and autopsies?*

Contarello   Yes. Knowing in advance means having a body to dig into. You say it all and then you write. What's the difference between knowing first and writing later? There's no difference.

Tozzi   *In some way, this has to do with the difference between the Jungian and the Freudian analytical vision. Freud mainly dug, and he dug to discover the causes of traumas and disorders, while Jung let the unconscious speak to him about something that not only came from the past, but also and most importantly for the future. Jung put consciousness and the unconscious on the same level, trusting the unconscious.*

Contarello   It is no coincidence that the narration of modern series is very Freudian as it tends to establish a moment, a scene, or anything else, which represents the ontological origin of what will happen afterwards.

Tozzi   *We have now reached the third phase of Active Imagination, that of recording of images transforming themselves. So far, we spoke about the manifesting of something we welcome and accept; something unknown that appears, becomes alive and takes a life of its own. This is the recording of transformation. A sort of objectifying imaginary contents, images, by giving them an expression through different modalities such as writing, music, painting, dance, sculpture, or any other form of expression.*

Contarello   By doing.

Tozzi   *Exactly. Representing what we have welcomed, seen, met and heard in a specific and personal expressive way. Writing seems to be your way of representing. But you recently discovered other forms of expression, like music.*

Contarello   Yes.

Tozzi   *I would like to know how you experience this third phase of Active Imagination, how you find it similar to your way of expressing ideas, meeting characters, stories.*

Contarello   Very easy! I am . . . one second!

Contarello [to Edoardo and Filippo]   Two pinches of salt.

Edoardo   Done!

Contarello [to Edoardo and Filippo]   Great. Now, open the Cantabrian anchovies, run them under cold water, put them on the cutting board – that big thing made of wood, it's easy to find – and then cut up an onion. As small as possible. Decide which one of you does it better.

Filippo   Ok!

Contarello   So, it's 2022 and I started working in 1985. Thirty-seven years spent creating the round shape, the story.

Tozzi   *Was it clear from the start? Did you always know that everything we've said – the fish that get caught in the net, the images that appear – had to be written?*

Contarello   No, I went through two phases. The first was neoclassical, meaning that I started working when cinema was made of a good story, good actors; live scenes didn't exist. The more classical authors were in the worst phase of their career. And comedy was awful. We could say we had lost all professions, from writing to filming, everything. So my career stems from a paradox: it was already old when it came to life, trying to recreate the neoclassic – neoclassic is classic. I grew up learning the neoclassic, which is a well-made story. I spent 30 years doing nothing else: at night, during the day, while having sex, I constantly thought about the perfect neoclassical story. At some point, because of personal reasons, because of my meeting with Paolo,[4] and mainly for the displacement of narrative cinema from the theater to the series, I approached it as a passion for cinema and not as a narrative form, as occurs in opera. Therefore, as the form of synthesis. When I speak of the opera I don't mean something incomprehensible or mysterious. No, I refer to the way of declining a story in the form of an opera. This is how I started idolizing Parise, my master. He is the only one who knows how to rape the cause and effect within a caption, to move toward a lyrical way of speaking. Just like Carlo Mazzacurati.[5] For those who always loved music, the following step is opera. Even for those who are tone deaf, the following step is to say, "I will now write a song". Songs are the perfect story, because instead of a structure which teaches, which is recognizable, which is the most important thing, they are also made of stanzas, chorus and final stanza. If I had to define what a story is, I could say it is a song. Just like you recognize a song from a leader or a symphony, you can recognize a story. A story follows the same dynamics; that is, a musical and not a narrative word, because it is made of repetitions of movements that go more and more in depth, until an opening and a return that finishes and weaves the threads. It is easier to explain what a story is by listening to "Yesterday" than explaining Aristotle. Much easier. When I start drafting a story, I choose a song that sounds like it.

Tozzi   *Like what?*

Contarello   For example I decide if . . .

Contarello [to Edoardo and Filippo]   You're still listening while cutting the onion, right?

Edoardo   We're here!

Contarello [to Edoardo and Filippo]   Good.

Filippo   We're cutting away!

Contarello   Great!

Contarello   For example, if there is some classicality, like the songs in the golden age of American music made by Europeans who migrated to the United States like Irving Berlin, George Gershwin, etc., therefore made of three stanzas, a chorus and two more stanzas; or a ballad. I always try to understand and decide beforehand if the story I sort of have in mind is more of a ballad or a song. If it's a song, I start listening to songs, if it's a ballad, I start listening to ballads.

Tozzi   So there is an interaction between music and writing which is therefore linked to poetry?

Contarello   Absolutely. According to the transitive property, if what you have in mind sounds like a ballad, you will find a poem that is a ballad, if it sounds like a song, you will find a poem that sounds like a song. What's the difference between narrated opera and narration? That the stanzas are narrating units and they are evocative, they have an emotional relationship with the following stanza, not a cause–effect relationship. All songs and music in general present this characteristic.

Tozzi   *It's fascinating: as you're speaking, I can hear, I see, I listen to what you're saying. It's a 3D experience!*

Contarello   If I want to draft a story set in Milan, I will listen very carefully to "Innamorati a Milano",[6] a song incredibly written, similar to Montale's poems. To say "in questo . . ." Ed. [in this . . .]. Wait, I want to be precise: if I say "sapessi" Ed. [if only you knew], everything else comes from that sentence, that implies something in between the real and imaginary.

Tozzi   *. . . and nostalgia.*

Contarello   Of course, and nostalgia. But also the desire to convince. The song says: "Sapessi com'è strano" Ed. [if only you knew how weird it is], referring to something quite normal like "darsi appuntamento a Milano" [meeting in Milan]. This sentence refers to the first act, for those who love the definition of first act. The word "sapessi" implies an attitude, an approach.

Tozzi   *An atmosphere.*

Contarello   There's an atmosphere.

Tozzi   *And therefore an environment. Both geographical and sentimental.*

Contarello   Exactly. And to say "In questo posto impossibile tu mi hai detto ti amo, io ti ho detto ti amo" Ed. [In this absurd place, you told me I love you, I told you I love you]. This is a purely lyrical passage, and it is in the chorus. So I know the chorus will be lyrical.

Tozzi   *Thank you, Umberto. We have reached the fourth and last phase of Active Imagination. According to Jung, this is the phase that truly makes up this methodology, or attitude. Adler, one of Jung's most well-known followers, believes – rightly so – that we shouldn't talk about "technique" of Active Imagination but rather attitude, and I think this is a fundamental clarification.*

Contarello   Yes. What you call attitude, I call approach, which is the same thing.

Tozzi   *I agree. According to Jung, this phase differentiates the attitude of Active Imagination from other methods to face the unconscious, and it is done through ethical comparison. The conscious ego talks with unconscious images and puts itself on the same level. It does not judge. At the same time, it takes a stance toward everything that emerged up until that moment, therefore toward images, their coming to life, evolving, and so on.*

Contarello   I perfectly understand. Hold on a moment, I need to check on those two.

Contarello [to Edoardo and Filippo]   So . . .

Filippo   We cut the onion.

Contarello [to Edoardo and Filippo]   Thin slices.

Edoardo   Yes.

Contarello [to Edoardo and Filippo]   Perfect. Now: last shelf on the right, get that pan – pan, not wok, even though it almost looks like a wok. Add a reasonable amount of oil. Turn on the smallest stove, low heat. Put the onion in the pan . . .

Edoardo   Mirepoix.

Contarello [to Edoardo and Filippo]   Yes, but remember: the onion needs to melt completely. If it starts burning, add some hot water. Hot, not cold!

Filippo   And the pasta?

Contarello [to Edoardo and Filippo]   Not yet.

Filippo   The water is boiling.

Contarello [to Edoardo and Filippo]   Ok, perfect! Now the onion needs to melt, then you add the anchovies and some hot water to try to make it creamy.

Edoardo   Creamy. Ok.

Contarello   Here I am.

Tozzi   *This shift between making pasta and Active Imagination, this alchemical process of cooking is pure poetry!*

Contarello   There is a text by Bruno Munari,[7] a genius, who used recipes as a procedure for fantasy. Today I asked Edoardo and Filippo: "Can you do me a favor? Let's cook something tonight and you will understand the process behind fantasy, because fantasy follows a procedure." When Munari writes a recipe he links every element of this phase to an element to grow fantasy. You were saying there is a comparison between consciousness and the unconscious, right?

Tozzi   *Yes. According to Jung, consciousness, the conscious ego, now faces everything that has emerged from the unconscious up until that point – images, events, contexts, situations. It doesn't expect to be superior and therefore to take over, as usually occurs in our conscious experience, when we negatively judge and underestimate. At the same time, the ego has a dialogue with the unconscious which leads it to taking a stance, to making a decision. How do you experience and feel this ethical comparison and how does it relate to your creating a story?*

Contarello   This is a hard question, because it hints that a part abandons itself and the other controls.

Tozzi   *They're on the same level.*

Contarello   Ok, they coexist.

Tozzi   *Yes.*

Contarello   That is actually my form of control, meaning that "I unconsciously do things and then I control them."

Tozzi   *No; then I talk to them and put myself out there. I put myself on the same level, I enter the scene and I dialogue. This is the main difference with other similar methods. For example, Jung often refers to meditation with talking about the first phase, that of letting things happen. The difference with meditation and other practices is that, in the case of Active Imagination, you don't remain passive – it is no coincidence it is called "active" – in front of everything that arrives. You* *start to give access to the unconscious, you welcome it. And then you put yourself out there, you talk and you take a stance.*

Contarello   This doesn't apply to me. After 30 years, my creations and fantasies are guided by control. There is no difference between the two. My fantasy is already assembled when it comes to life.

Tozzi   *No, wait: the fourth phase does not necessarily come after the others. With a good practice of Active Imagination they can also co-exist.*

Contarello   I turned this the other way around. In my case, invention contains. Usually, fantasy is unconscious and control conscious. In my case, it's the opposite. My unconscious is controlled since I practiced it for years. I know my fantasy has an impact on stanzas, chorus and final stanza. That is the unconscious, the controlled part is conscious because this is what I'm used to. I haven't spent one moment in the past 37 years without thinking about creating, which has therefore become unconscious. My fantasy is already assembled, I don't need to go in there and put it together. I don't have a third eye that judges if fantasy follows an order, because it already comes to life with order, composed. My problem is actually breaking this composition. My third eye doesn't control but breaks the habits I perceive as old. What we could refer to as "the way".

Tozzi   *You said it has to do with the definition of attitude. When an attitude of Active Imagination is inbuilt, there is no separation between the phases, with no need to rationally explain them: it just happens. And what about the dialogue with your characters?*

Contarello   Nonsense, come on! No one talks to their characters. We all just dialogue with ourselves!

Tozzi   *Of course, that's exactly what I mean. The imaginary representation of the contents of your unconscious, with whom you can dialogue. You therefore dialogue with yourself.*

Contarello   But it is never fully rational, clear.

Tozzi   *You are somewhere in between.*

Contarello   I am a sleep-walker.

Tozzi   *Exactly, you're somewhere in between.*

Contarello   Yes.

Tozzi   *This is what Jung refers to in the fourth phase of Active Imagination. This is what he means when he talks about a dialogue between two equals. There is no superior or inferior, no controller and controlled. It is a matter of being somewhere in between, a very special experience.*

Contarello   It is very similar to when you wake up at night and you can only use your hands to move around. My desire to write comes from feeling lost.

Tozzi   *And the faithful abandonment, as in the beginning of Active Imagination.*

Contarello   Exactly! This is something I achieved.

Tozzi   *Yes!*

Contarello   It was hard.

Tozzi   *I can imagine!*

Contarello   I know I can walk into a theater with 5,000 people and say, "Give me five words and I will tell you a story with those five words," because I know how to do it. But I do it if I'm being paid, I don't do it at home. I don't do this with my students. I tell them things that have a feeling, an understanding.

Tozzi   *Finally, feelings! Jung talks about feelings referring to the experience of Active Imagination.*

Contarello   Of course.

Tozzi   Compared to a logical attitude which is therefore lacking feeling and that is typical of the ego.

Contarello   Understanding has to do with control.

Tozzi   *Exactly.*

Contarello   And the fear of not having control. I am Narcissus. There are very few papers on this: Narcissus is not afraid of losing control because he is married to himself and therefore, he is confident.

Tozzi   *If this didn't exist, nobody would trust themselves.*

Contarello   Yes, but it has to be authentic. If it is not, it is a tragedy.
Contarello [to Edoardo and Filippo]   It smells good! Are the onions are almost completely melted, almost . . .
Edoardo   *Impalpable?*
Contarello [to Edoardo and Filippo]   Impalpable. And shooting for the clouds.
Filippo   Amazing.

Tozzi   *I think we can end here. It was amazing. We started by talking about synchronicity, we mentioned faithful abandonment and reached the impalpable clouds.*

Contarello   Which is nothing more than an onion!

Tozzi   *What more could we want!?*

Contarello   It's like matter that becomes air. The problem is turning it into air.

Tozzi   *Air and smell.*

Contarello   Yes, air and smell!

Notes

1 Fabrizio De Andrè is one of the most well-known Italian singer-songwriters (Ed.).
2 Dr. Mario Trevi, Italian Jungian analyst, CIPA-IAAP (Ed.).
3 Dr. Francesco Montanari, Italian Jungian analyst, CIPA-IAAP (Ed.).
4 Paolo Sorrentino, Italian Director (Ed.).
5 Carlo Mazzacurati, Italian Director (Ed.).
6 *Innamorati a Milano* (1965), by Memo Remigi and Alberto Testa.
7 Munari, B. (1981). *Da cosa nasce cosa*. Editore: Laterza.

Chapter 10

Bridges, Hybrids and Devils

Floating in a Movie with Jung

Mario Sesti

Is the imaginary a socially shared repository of images that works both as an encyclopedia capable of regulating and directing internal pathways and as a device for preserving and producing them? Is the imaginary a repository of clichés or the set made of a mysterious energy that can make them explode and perpetually evolve and transform? Is it a selective advantage that allows the human species to play and experiment with alternatives to the real? Is it a receptacle of plots and incomplete relationships and figures that every narrative aims to integrate? Is it a place of contamination and encounter, hybridization and negotiation of consciousness and the unconscious? Before Jung turned imagination into the activity capable of leading the Ego-consciousness to explore the immensity of the unconscious, a great philosopher, Kant, had already made it the crucial coordination of distant regions of the empire of humanity, sensibility and intellect, ascribing to it the decisive functionality of transcendental schematism. This is exactly what allows our perceptions of objects in space and time to be linked by cause–effect, and all our representations (which are nothing more than images generated by our encounter with the real, or by our imagination, which in Kant is always reproductive) to arrange themselves endlessly in the transition of our consciousness in the narration of the order of things, of days, of seasons, wrenching the Ego out of the chaos of dreams or the madness resulting from the non-existence of a unifying principle of the irreparable multiplicity of the real. Imagination is the place of maximum condensation of images and things, its terrain vague, the permanent laboratory of something because it is never something; that ember in the fireplace that continues to burn even when the fire has been out for hours, its reddish pulsations radiating through the room even when everyone is in bed, its heat floating in the air even when no one is there to enjoy it.

According to Antonio Damasio, one of the most influential and innovative contemporary neuroscientists, there are few things like cinema that resemble our consciousness. According to the scientist, the way this language of images and sounds, created at the end of the 1900s, has perfected technologies, narrative functions, styles of expression and production of meaning – actually the same ones that are casually used today by teenagers to post a video on TikTok, even if invented by Chaplin – closely resembles the way our mind and body system registers, selects,

DOI: 10.4324/9781003411383-10

orders and "edits" all the data produced by our nervous system's encounters with the world. Every thought is a fragment of the imagination of a desire, the most extreme and schematic synthesis of psychoanalysis; every film is the transposition of that chain of transmission from the world to the consciousness that produces thoughts. It is a karstic and underground creative passage thanks to which images, like thermal waters, are loaded with slag, matter, symbolic debris, fragments of meaning, archetypal figures, traumatic inscriptions, millenary deposits of fossilized narratives. The power of the image, and the power of imagination, is to limit all heterogeneity to a transparent identity. The surface of an image never shows the infinite chain of articulations, sutures, mutations, grafts; that is, the seismic tumult that produced it and that now, hidden, lies below its crystal-clear integrity.

"Politicians tell us that the countries and nations we live in are unique, while movies tell us that there are no boundaries." This premise, almost at the opening of the documentary, *The Story of Film: A New Generation* by Mark Cousins, is nearly enough to invite us on a truly special and precious journey through that movement; thought, language, made of images and sounds to which, over a century ago, we learned to refer with one word: cinema.

It is a journey that Cousins began several years ago with a 15-part documentary series called *The Story of Film: An Odyssey*. This extract, presented in 2021 at the Cannes Classics, over 2 hours long, is the last episode. Which films and writers in recent seasons of the silver screen have intelligently and passionately extended the possibilities of the very form of cinema? Cousins himself points them out to us. What I consider particularly significant is that this list – which includes some of the directors with the most personal, refined and challenging style, the most innovative and extreme forms – includes a so-called blockbuster, a very successful genre film that Cousins puts on the same level as those the most cerebral writers. The title is *Mad Max: Fury Road*. To understand the reasons behind this choice we will try, as an exercise related to the topic we are interested in, to break down and analyze the images of this film, which technically belongs to the dystopian science fiction genre, one that has proliferated, for example, on on-demand platforms, but that also has a long and respectable background of traditional literary science fiction. Films of this type tell us about life once the world we know and belong to is no more.

The film begins by introducing a little girl's voice-over with production signs and stock footage. Within seconds, it describes the way the world we know has ended: climate catastrophes, social crises, the system falling apart. When we see a man in the foreground grabbing a reptile and stuffing it into his mouth, we realize that the girl's voice we were listening to was in his head. The man, the protagonist of the film, is a former policeman. The little girl was his daughter, whom he was unable to save from violent death as a result of the world crisis that led to the extinction of civilization. We realize this immediately afterwards when we see the onslaught of jeeps driven by screaming warriors, colored like Native Americans, chasing the ex-policeman who is trying to escape them in his car. The chase is the film's main narrative figure; it is the way through which cinema began to develop its own narrative syntax. Before cinema, in theater, or in a book, it was neither easy nor interesting to tell the story of two individuals chasing one another. Cinema turned this proto-history into an inexhaustible source of images and narratives, making the very idea of the chase so popular and dominant to the point that, in the United States and elsewhere, "cut to the chase" has become a common way of saying "get to the point". In some ways, all of *Mad Max* works with highly intel-lectualized techniques of stylization on primordial forms of imagination and sto-rytelling: how to use the latest technology to work on millenary geological areas. Imagination casts its probes with cutting-edge technology to reach the abysses of the unconscious.

Max, the protagonist, is soon captured and made prey in the residence of a mon-arch with prehistoric costumes who lives inside a stronghold over a canyon. Es-sentially, Max has become a pool of blood to be injected as needed into one of the warriors surrounding the king in this patriarchal tyranny that seems to be based pre-cisely on the possession of the goods that are most at risk today: water, fossil fuel, women as passive reproduction tools. So far, the whole style of the film appears to be an excellent performance of the greatest specialization of American cinema (cinema as action, the sequence as a synthesis of intermittent points of intensity, violence as the primary focus of the eye). But this performance is staged with the original force of subjectivity, the first requirement for auteur cinema: colors are processed with great sensuality (expanses of yellow deserts, amber-colored rocks, wild meadows, glacial complexions), the mix of prehistory and mechanical tech-nology gives every shot a sense of persuasion. The promiscuity of warrior bodies and deformed dwarves, warlike aristocracy and masses of dispossessed people, is the epic backdrop to the creation of this world. The body is the first parameter we will examine.

A few minutes into the movie, there are a handful of shots through which the film's imagination (the action of images) harpoons the collective unconscious. The Demon Monarch, a sort of priestly patriarch who dominates everybody in the realm, including the daughters he abuses at his own will, for several generations, at some point catches the attention of the crowds of dispossessed people gathered at the bottom of the canyon. They are walking, skeletal and catatonic-looking bodies advancing towards the base of the vertical spur from which the Demon Patriarch addresses them, waiting for something. Their steps are unsteady, the rags they wear are miserable, their gaze is dull and opaque. That mass of malnourished bodies, advancing half-heartedly, recalls the first of the great archetypal images of contemporaneity. I have shown this scene dozens of times to my students, aspir-ing scriptwriters and young critics, and when I ask them "What does this image remind you of?", regardless of their age or the context of the lesson, class or city, there is always at least one person who says: "The Holocaust". Since the 1900s, that image (the emptied bodies, the inanimate gaze, the catatonic infirmity, form-ing a mass) has been strongly connected to the greatest fear: being exterminated by an unstoppable power. In cinema, the action of images (imagination) has the power to connect us to our greatest fears, to their never-ending storage, without naming them.

A similar analysis could be carried out for many other narrative and visual configurations, of which the film is full. The main characters are warriors whose dream is to die in battle to reach the "Walhalla", a name reminiscent of the Adila of Northern European myths. They are actually suicide bombers whose final goal is to reach the afterlife by taking on a bloody sacrifice. Do we need to mention the great fear such a fantasy could cause after 9/11? But it is even more interesting to analyze how imagination overturns real data; it manipulates it, hybridizes it, turns it into an object of creative intention. These suicide bombers have nothing to do with the Koran, their battle cry is metal music. The most flagrant and unprecedented visual impact of the film is the populated shot of a fleet of vehicles over which, like the war horns of the armies of the ancient world, guitarists in a state of war trance are chasing with the scream of their distorted solos against the backdrop of the jet of flamethrowers. Who gave life to these images, and why? What is the power that makes them both intriguing and disturbing? Interestingly, the work of imagination has to take us back to reality, transforming it, in some ways overturning it. The music these warriors use to refill and reach states of individual and collective excitement is of the same genre as that played at the Bataclan in Paris where authentic Islamic suicide bombers killed hundreds of people to stage their hatred of a lifestyle somehow represented by the love for that music. What strikes me as most surprising is the bricolage with which active imagination constructs figures through even inconsistent pieces of the unconscious. It is also a sign of its freedom, the true source of its power. The imagery of metal is grotesque, horrific and in some ways violent (in lyrics, in attitudes; more rarely in reality). Miller hybridizes it with one of the most widespread fears of contemporaneity (the homicidal and suicidal acts of terrorism), precisely building that bridge between consciousness and the unconscious, individual consciousness and collective imagination, capable of negotiating a contact and an exchange, a contamination that sharpens our sensitivity, arouses our perceptions and nourishes our intelligence with the pleasure of a creativity. In a seductive way, it brings buried internal discourses to the surface. Cinema, like the most unscrupulous politicians, knows that the most effective way to communicate is to connect us with our oldest feeling: fear. The same feeling that probably allowed us to populate the planet. That same fear that made great mammals like the saber-toothed tiger disappear – we were their favorite prey. *Mad Max* was a hit all over the world, and even though it was first and foremost imagined for that reason (profits), with its compositional style reminding us of Dali, the memorable originality of the creation of bodies in front of the frame (an authentic fusion of make-up design, set design, costumes), the energy of its treatment of themes (the crisis of the environment, the fear of terrorism) is confirmation of what film critics argued somewhat provocatively in the 1970s: the only true political cinema is genre cinema; as shown in the last meaningful segment, that we will only briefly mention, but which is the real driving force behind the film's entire narrative.

Mad Max is about a former police officer who failed to protect his daughter and ends up escorting a crew of women who fled from a tyrannical, violent and rapist patriarch. It is a 2015 film; the #MeToo movement officially began in 2017 with a tweet from Alyssa Milano urging every woman to go public with the violence they had been subjected to. It is hard to find a more persuasive example of the world in which the imagination of cinema intercepts the collective imagination. In his beautiful documentary film mentioned above, with the same throbbing emotion of someone who is about to share a secret or a discovery, Cousins' voice flips through every genre, from comedy to documentary to musical, to show us how a hieratic Thai director like Apichatpong creates the metaphor of sleep and dreams in a hospital ward or a shopping mall; how Leos Carax does it in *Holy Motors*; how an Indian gangster film (*Gangs of Wasseypur*) hybridizes crime with dance. In every corner of the world, from California to Estonia, from the deserts of Namibia where *Mad Max* was filmed, which has the innovative power of colors, editing and storytelling of an art-house film, to the Chinese interiors of a film of pure and unrepeatable psychic and social extremism like *An Elephant Sitting Still* (whose writer, Hu Bo, committed suicide before the premiere of his work), from the hyper-technological Africa reinvented by Marvel in *Black Panther* to the feminist science fiction of *Gravity*, from Godard to Ari Aster. In every square meter of the planet where a video camera is placed or a GoPro is mounted, Cousins shows us that, if you take away the economics of massive investments, the star system, the tireless gossip, what remains of cinema is creativity and care, the skill of innovation of form and the obsession with tumult or the unreal stillness of life in images: tumult, obsession and skill that I have the impression may be precisely what fascinated Jung's imagination.

References

Cousins, Mark. *The Story of Film: An Odyssey* [Documentary], Hopscotch Films, 2011.
Cousins, Mark. *The Story of Film: A New Generation* [Documentary], Hopscotch Films, 2021.
Damasio, Antonio. "Cinema, esprit ed éemotion: la perspective du cervau", *Trafic*, 67, autumn 2008.
Mad Max: Fury Road [Film], Dir. George Miller, Warner Bros., 2015.
Sobchack, Vivian. *Carnal Thoughts: Embodiement and Moving Image Culture*, University of California Press, Berkeley, 2004.
Thomson, David. *How To Watch a Movie*, Profile Books, Croydon, 2016.

Chapter 11

Exploring the Active Search for Information During Active Imagination

Gianfranca Nieddu and Irene Cogliatti Dezza

Introduction

Acknowledging that the training offered by the Jungian Psychoanalytic Community considerably lacks a theoretical and clinical-practical focus on what Jung considered one of his cornerstones of therapeutic methodology, i.e. Active Imagination, the authors suggest an observational area for empirical and experimental research where to further analyze the imaginal attitude of consciousness and the benefits that can be obtained at the clinical level through the use of Active Imagination. By doing so, the authors present a novel cognitive look at Jungian thought where the active search for information that occurred during Active Imagination is investigated, opening up to further investigations into the neural basis involved in such a therapeutic approach, while preserving and respecting the complexity of the human psyche and analytical psychology, avoiding one-sided explanations and in line with new scientific interpretations.

Images and Imagination as an Active Process

The center of Jung's thought has always been images and imagination both considered as an "active" method of psychic introspection. In his book *Memories, Dreams, Reflections* (1961) we can already see the potential ascribed to images:

> The years when I was pursuing my inner images were the most important in my life – in them everything essential was decided. It all began then; the later details are only supplements and clarifications of the material that burst forth from the unconscious, and at first swamped me. It was the *prima materia* for a lifetime's work.[1]

Although the scientific community has acknowledged Jung's pioneering attention to the faculty of imagination, it has only done so partially, setting aside the central core identified by Jung himself, that is, the *practice of an active dialogue* between the Ego-consciousness and the unconscious contents that surface from imagination.

DOI: 10.4324/9781003411383-11

In Jungian analytical therapy there is a tendency to favor the emergence of psychic images as such, becoming aware and using them to obtain a cathartic effect that replaces a literal interpretation with a symbolic reading/understanding of the contents represented in images. However, there is often a tendency to limit the special dialogue that takes place by virtue of Active Imagination, necessary to ensure a constructive and transformative encounter between the conscious and the unconscious. On the contrary, Jung considered the possibility of activating an ethical comparison between the Ego and the unconscious as the *via regia* to favor the emergence of a symbolic attitude of the mind, capable of activating the transcendent function aimed at overcoming psychic opposites (rational/irrational, conscious/ unconscious, high/low, etc.). Therefore, following Jungian thought in the approach to imagination – but also with the interpretation of dreams or through the use of "sandplay", albeit with specific differences – we cannot simply limit ourselves to a contemplative and/or interpretative use, both literally and symbolically, of the images that come from the unconscious; we must ensure an active participation of the Ego and the possibility of it placing itself symmetrically and not above the unconscious. Thus, the attention given to the phenomena of the psychic unconscious allows us to understand how the Ego-consciousness is not to be seen as a "superior entity" but as a fundamental *entity* to symmetrically address the dialogue and ethical comparison with the unconscious and its manifestations. The result of this comparison leads to a psychic transformation given by the comparison and integration of opposing contents, where both the contents of the conscious Ego and of the unconscious can converge, favoring the achievement of a new plan of imaginal awareness.

The Four Phases of Jung's Active Imagination

Active Imagination is a process of dialogue between the conscious and the unconscious, one of the most important steps in the individuation process as differentiation in the search for individuality. In this complex process, Jung creates the concept of "transcendent function". According to Dallett,[2] Active Imagination is the most important method to develop and activate the transcendent function. Jung inherited the assumption of an active role with regard to inner images from the alchemical tradition, where there was already a clear distinction between *Phantasia*, i.e. a passive enjoyment of fantasizing, and *Vera imaginatio*, where, on the contrary, an ethical comparison was required to ask and respond to the images that appear.[3] Through an imaginal dialogue between the conscious Ego and the figures of the unconscious, and the contents of the individual and collective unconscious, the Jungian method of Active Imagination falls within this perspective, giving rise to a new ethical and cognitive attitude that favors the path of individuation. Active Imagination, the dialogue between the *Ego* and the *unconscious*, is central to Jungian analytical psychology (often not adequately analyzed in-depth) and finds its highest expression in the *Red Book*.[4] By using images extrapolated from his inner listening, Jung makes the individual and collective archetypal contents of the psyche "visible and objectifiable", also through the use of figurative and colorful representations.

To this day, the content of this extraordinary and complex work is studied with fear and is seen as controversial. According to M.L. Von Franz,[5] the process of Active Imagination develops according to four phases.

Phase 1: Emptying of the Mind

Emptying of the mind is common to many meditation traditions in their initial phase. After reaching a state of relaxation, consciousness empties, trying to make it impervious to interference from the conscious Ego and the external environment:

> letting things happen, action through non-action, letting go of oneself as taught by Meister Eckhart, became for me the key that opens the door to the way. We must be able to let things happen in the psyche. For us, this is an art of which most people know nothing. Consciousness is forever interfering, helping, correcting, and negating, never leaving the psychic processes to grow in peace.[6]

Phase 2: Letting the Psychic Event Happen; The Pregnant Image

> In this way a new attitude is created, an attitude that accepts the irrational and the incomprehensible simply because it is happening.[7]

In phase 2, it is important for Jung to take in the images, paying attention to them, even and especially to what is irrational and incomprehensible. It is important to look at the images without a critical attitude:

> So to look at or concentrate upon a thing, betrachten, gives the quality of being pregnant to the object. And if it is pregnant, then something is due to come out of it; it is alive, it produces, it multiplies.[8]

In the commentary to *The Secret of the Golden Flower* (1929), Jung associates this phase with the "wu-wei" concept of the Taoists, not to interfere with the natural flow of things.[9] Let things happen (*geschehenlassen*), welcome them, and focus on what emerges (*betrachten*).

Phase 3: Objectification

The third phase is the moment when the image is given an external expression through the main forms of art (reading, writing, photography, dance, music); it is enriched with details and can evolve, develop and transform itself. This trans-formation must not go too far in aesthetic processing or result in an exaggerated formalism. Active Imagination is a unique method and it can be expressed in different ways.

Phase 4: Ethical Comparison with the Unconscious

The first three phases mentioned above and conventionally used to describe the method of Active Imagination are not only related to Active Imagination; in fact, it is possible to find similar phases in other more traditional forms of meditation.

The last phase, full of meaning and specificity of the Jungian method, is that of ethical comparison with what emerges from the unconscious; the Ego actively enters into the experience, consciousness takes the lead. It is the phase of intuitions, questions of meaning, doubts and moral demands.[10]

Objectives

Our study stems from the observation that, during the analytical path of individuation and through the use of Active Imagination, intense inner listening takes place, interesting both conscious and unconscious aspects; the transcendent function is the key element, accompanied by great individual emotional engagement based upon activation. The goals of this work are to gain insights into this process in which the analysand is actively searching for internal information and the benefits that can be obtained at a clinical level thanks to this active search. Paving the way to this understanding will both promote a greater use of Active Imagination in the analytical psychotherapy and individuate possible neuronal pathways involved.

Methodology

To gain insights into the active search for internal information that occurred during Active Imagination, we first administered a semi-structured interview to a heterogeneous group of professionals in terms of age, gender and cultural background, who had all attended Jungian training and underwent Active Imagination sessions. The aim of these interviews was to identify internal operating methods common to several individuals in order to guide us during the preparation of a more structured questionnaire (see below). During the interviews, we let the professionals talk freely about their experience with Active Imagination. However, we ensured that a few topics were discussed: why they decided to approach Active Imagination, the ways they encountered Active Imagination, the emotions connected to this pathway, the possible transformations at the emotional and/or physical level, and the possible changes that occurred in the short-, medium- and long-term, at the expense of internal and external operational choices. Based on the responses collected during these interviews, we prepared a specific questionnaire and delivered it to 35 professionals. Such a questionnaire, while not providing a total score, allowed us to highlight the process through which the active search for internal information takes place and possible therapeutic benefits that can emerge by allowing such a search. The questionnaire consisted of 18 items, divided into three main areas:

- A first section dedicated to personal data collection (age, gender etc.).
- A central exploratory section (Items 4–6) with regard to Active Imagination: how and the extent to which this method was known to analysts (Jungian and non-Jungian); whether they had previous experiences of analytic therapy or psychotherapy; whether they had ever approached Active Imagination and the effects experienced psychically or physically following the encounter with Active Imagination.
- A third and final section (items 7–18) based on the emotional and practical considerations that arose from that encounter with Active Imagination and any changes brought about by such an encounter. In particular, Items 7 to 13 are ones that favor inner exploration, while items 14 to 18 concern the relapse of the effects of Active Imagination on the outside world.

Results

First, we observed that when exposed to the four main phases of Active Imagination, all, or almost all, individuals we interviewed went through similar active research for information. Through personal and different exploratory steps, they reached conclusions that were certainly individual but also similar in terms of operational choices, acquiring awareness and reducing clinical symptoms. In the sample observed, the method of Active Imagination allowed a greater balance and the fastest access to unconscious information, collective and individual experiences, proving to be, for almost all the individuals observed, a powerful therapeutic tool.

Next, we administered the 18-item questionnaire to 35 individuals (average age 42; 29 females and 6 males). In the aforementioned sample, 100 percent had had at least one previous experience of analytical psychotherapy, but only 40 percent had had direct experience of Active Imagination. We then selected only participants who had had a direct experience with Active Imagination (40 percent of total sample; average age 40; 71 percent female and 29 percent male). The most significant outcome was related to the questions aimed at investigating emotional involvement: almost all of the sample investigated (99 percent) experienced significant emotional involvement during and after their encounter with Active Imagination; 90 percent of the professionals who filled in the questionnaire also confirmed that they were able to reach awareness more quickly when faced with events that had hitherto remained in the shadow. Likewise, 80 percent of the sample noticed a greater access to unconscious information, both collective and individual experiences; 71 percent of the sample confirmed that their experience of Active Imagination allowed them to confront the unconscious on their own, continuing to work with the images produced during the following experience of Active Imagination.

This made it possible to highlight how the analysand was able to learn and pursue an individual pathway even in the analyst's absence. A very similar percentage of individuals stated that, following such an experience, they noticed changes with regard to inner and external relationships with, for example, patients, collaborators and colleagues. Although the limited size of the sample requires us to be cautious, as repeatedly mentioned, it should be noted that some clinical aspects have improved following an experience of Active Imagination in terms of greater awareness and less "pressure" of clinical symptoms. In this regard, the somatoform or free anxious aspects improved, as well as some related to depressive aspects of the mood and the phobic-anxiety spectrum.

Discussion

The aim of this study was to highlight a novel observational area for empirical and experimental research to better understand the active search for internal information that occurred during Active Imagination and possible therapeutic benefits of such a therapeutic approach. Our results collectively suggest that, through this active search, a faster access to unconscious information occurred as well as an increased emotional engagement and an improvement of both anxiety and mood-related symptoms. With the help of semi-structured interviews, we identified the internal operating methods common to the interviewed participants during Active Imagination sessions. Such common internal operations included a greater balance and faster access to unconscious information.

We better explored these operations using an 18-item questionnaire. Results from this questionnaire suggested that participants were able to reach awareness more quickly; they also noticed a greater access to unconscious information and enhanced emotional engagement.

By showing that Active Imagination allows individuals to quickly search for unconscious information, hypotheses can be drawn on the neural basis of such a therapeutic approach. In particular, the neural networks involved when humans search for information[11] might be potential candidates for such mechanisms. For example, pre-frontal regions such as the dorsal anterior cingulate cortex and deep brain regions such as the basal ganglia, activated when people search for information in their external space,[12] might sustain the active search for information during Active Imagination. Recent studies indeed suggest that the search for internal information and the search for information in the external space share similar neural mechanisms.[13] Future studies, however, are needed to test this hypothesis by applying brain-imaging techniques during Active Imagination sessions.

Exploring the neural substrates involved in Active Imagination might also better inform about the therapeutic benefits of this approach. In our study, most of the participants reported a decrease in symptoms at the clinical level, thanks to the ability to transform their internal operational choices. In particular, almost the entire sample showed positive changes with regard to the phobic-anxiety and mood-related symptoms. Therefore, Active Imagination might be used as a therapeutic tool to reduce symptoms and improve patients' mental health. Most importantly, participants also reported that Active Imagination allowed them to confront the unconscious on their own, allowing them to learn and pursue an individual pathway even in the absence of the analyst. This is a key point of this therapeutic approach that can be used by patients on their own to reduce their symptoms on a daily basis. Further research is, however, needed to extend these findings to a larger sample of participants, where symptoms are measured using DSM-V criteria and/or validated psychopathological questionnaires.

Despite the potential benefits of Active Imagination, our study also showed a lack of more in-depth knowledge of the use and potential of Active Imagination as a therapeutic approach, especially in analysts who recently attended Jungian training. Indeed, a significant number of colleagues (60 percent) who had given their availability to take the questionnaire were not able to continue the study as they had no direct personal experience of Active Imagination (both during the training and afterwards).

Conclusion

The lack of scientific data, the high specificity of the method of Active Imagination and, above all, the strong emotional involvement needed for its application could partly justify the minimal implementation and importance given to this method, Jungian *par excellence*, especially in training. Moreover, it must be emphasized that the analysis of the results reported here is only descriptive and remains open to new research possibilities. Although not based on a numerically significant sample and obtained through a non-standardized and purely observational questionnaire, these observations appear to be in line with what is reported in the literature and suggest how, by taking on an "attitude of Active Imagination", the ability to profoundly transform the way we relate to both the internal and external world can be improved. Despite the above-mentioned limitations, the results encourage greater educational dissemination and use at clinical level, at least by the Jungian scientific community, and support the possibility of researching neuroscientific correlates both in more statistically structured terms and by using brain-imaging techniques.

Notes

1 Jung C.G., 1961, *Memories, Dreams, Reflections*. London: Fontana Press, 1995, Ch. VI, p. 137.
2 Dallett, J., "Active Imagination in practice", in Stein, M. (Ed.), *Jungian Analysis*. Open Court, La Salle & London, 1982.
3 Jung C.G. "Mysterium coniunctionis", in *Collected Works of C.G. Jung*, Vol. 14; Bollati Boringhieri, 1991.
4 Jung C.G. *Il libro Rosso* [The Red Book], 9th ed., Bollati Boringhieri, 2010.

5 Von Franz, M.L. "L'immaginazione attiva" [The active imagination], *Rivista di psicologia analitica* [Journal of Analytical Psychology], 17, 1978.
6 Jung, C.G., "Conscious, Unconscious and Individuation". *Collected Works 9/1.* Princeton, NJ: Princeton University Press, 1939 (Jung, 1960/1969).
7 Ibid.
8 Ibid.
9 Jung C.G., *Commento al* Segreto del fiore d'oro [Commentary to *The Secret of the Golden Flower*] (1929/1957). Prefazione di C.G. Jung [Preface by C.G. Jung], 2nd ed., 1938.
10 Jung C.G., *Jung on Active Imagination*. J. Chodorow, Ed., Princeton University Press, 1997.
11 Charpentier C., Cogliati Dezza, I., "Information-seeking in the brain". In Cogliati Dezza, I., Schulz, E., Wu, C. (Eds.), *The Drive for Knowledge: The Science of Human Information-Seeking*, Cambridge University Press, 2022. Cogliati Dezza, I., Cleeremans, A., Alexander, W., "Independent and interacting value system for reward and information in the human brain". *eLife*, 11, e66358, 2022; Kobayashi, K., Hsu, M., "Common neural code for reward and information value", *PNAS*, 116(26): 13061–13066, 2019; Charpentier, C.J., Bromberg-Martin, E., Sharot, T. (2018) "Valuation of knowledge and ignorance in mesolimbic reward circuitry". *PNAS*, 115(31): E7255–E7264.
12 Charpentier, Cogliati Dezza, "Information-seeking in the brain"; Cogliati Dezza, Cleeremans, Alexander, "Independent and interacting value system for reward and information in the human brain".
13 Hills, T.T., Lundin, N.B., Luthra, M., Todd, P.M., "Seeking inner knowledge". In Cogliati Dezza, I., Schulz, E., Wu, C. (Eds.), *The Drive for Knowledge: The Science of Human Information-Seeking*, Cambridge University Press, 2022.

References

Charpentier, C., Cogliati Dezza, I. (2022) "Information-seeking in the brain". In Cogliati Charpentier, C.J., Bromberg-Martin, E., Sharot, T. (2018), "Valuation of knowledge and ignorance in mesolimbic reward circuitry". *PNAS*, 115(31): E7255–E7264.

Cogliati Dezza, I., Cleeremans, A., Alexander, W. (2022) "Independent and interacting value system for reward and information in the human brain". *eLife*, 11: e66358.

Dallett, J. (1982) "Active Imagination in practice", in Stein, M. (Ed.), *Jungian Analysis*. La Salle & London: Open Court.

Dezza, I., Schulz, E., Wu C. (Eds.), *The Drive for Knowledge: The Science of Human Information-Seeking*. Cambridge: Cambridge University Press.

Hills, T.T., Lundin, N.B., Luthra, M., Todd, P.M. (2022) "Seeking inner knowledge". In Cogliati Dezza, I., Schulz, E., Wu, C. (Eds.), *The Drive for Knowledge: The Science of Human Information-Seeking*. Cambridge: Cambridge University Press.

Jung, C.G. (1938) Commento al *Segreto del fiore doro* [Commentary to *The Secret of the Golden Flower*] (1929/1957). Prefazione di C.G. Jung [Preface by C.G. Jung], 2nd ed. Turin: Bollati Boringhieri.

Jung, C.G. (1939) "Conscious, unconscious and individuation". *Collected Works 9/1.* Princeton, NJ: Princeton University Press (Jung, 1960/1969).

Jung C.G. (1961) *Memories, Dreams, Reflections*. London: Fontana Press, 1995.

Jung C.G. (1965) *Ricordi, Sogni, Riflessioni* [Memories, Dreams, Reflections], 1st ed. Milan: Il Saggiatore.

Jung C.G. (1991) "Mysterium coniunctionis", in *Collected Works of C.G. Jung*, vol. 14. Turin: Bollati Boringhieri.

Jung C.G. (1997) *Jung on Active Imagination*. J. Chodorow, Ed. Princeton, NJ: Princeton University Press.

Jung, C.G. (2010) *Il libro Rosso* [The Red Book], 9th ed. Turin: Bollati Boringhieri.

Kobayashi, K., Hsu, M. (2019) "Common neural code for reward and information value". *PNAS*, 116(26): 13061–13066.

Von Franz, M.L. (1978) "L'immaginazione attiva" [The active imagination], in *Rivista di psicologia analitica* [Journal of Analytical Psychology], 17.

Chapter 12

Active Imagination and Quantum Entanglement

An Outlook

Emiliano Puddu

A wide disquisition on the analogies between Quantum Physics and analytical psychology, and in particular on synchronicity, can be found in the collection of letters between the psychoanalyst Carl Gustav Jung and the physicist Wolfgang Pauli (Meier, 2001). In this chapter I will show an analogy between the technique of active imagination and the phenomenon of quantum entanglement. In particular, I will expose how active imagination could be seen from the the point of view of Quantum Mechanics and the importance that it has in our lives from this perspective. I must point out that there is no formal overlap between the fields of Jungian psychology and Quantum Mechanics, and that I only investigate a possible analogy between them. Lastly, I will present a direct experience from my life.

C.G. Jung proposed a map of the human psyche, which is composed of two parts: the conscious and the unconscious. In particular, the latter would be much wider than the first, and would not be empty at birth, but would contain elements common to all human beings, as well as those familiar and personal. This map of the psyche is represented in different ways, all having in common the fact that the conscious component of the psyche is smaller in size than that of the unconscious. The unconscious itself can be represented by different layers developing under the conscious mind: the personal unconscious contains memories of experiences removed by the Ego, that are no longer acceptable; the collective unconscious is a heritage whose contents are common to all human beings and here reside the archetypes that accompanied the human being in his history.

While the Self has access to the entire Psyche, "the ego is, by definition, subordinate to the self and is related to it like a part to the whole" (*Collected Works 9*, Jung, 1969: 5). In the same work, Jung states that "the more numerous and the more significant the unconscious contents which are assimilated to the ego, the closer the approximation of the ego to the self, even though this approximation must be a never- ending process" (ibid.). This never-ending process can be facilitated by the active imagination. Active imagination allows one to become acquainted with the archetypes and unconscious contents of the psyche, without the need to give an analytical explanation. In particular, Jung defines the transcendent function "as a quality of conjoined opposites" (*Collected Works 8*, Jung, 1960: 127). During

DOI: 10.4324/9781003411383-12

active imagination the Ego comes into contact with the unconscious world through images and symbolic contents. The encounter between conscious and unconscious contents opens the door to individuation and to the Self.

In Collected Works 18, ¶1554, Jung introduces the transcendent function as that function of the Psyche able to mend the separation between the conscious and unconscious mind: "The cooperation of conscious reasoning with the data of the unconscious is called the "transcendent function. (. . .) This function progressively unites the opposites. (. . .) Besides this, it is a natural and spontaneous phenomenon, part of the process of individuation."

Active imagination can be introduced by four main stages, first proposed by Marie-Louise Von Franz (1980):

1. Empty the mad mind of the Ego;
2. Let the unconscious fantasy image arise;
3. Give it some form of expression;
4. Ethical confrontation.

To explain better the analogy between active imagination and the phenomenon of Quantum Mechanics, I need to provide the reader with some information about Physics.

In Quantum Mechanics, a physical quantity that can be measured in any way, directly or indirectly, is defined as observable. Recall that a physical quantity is a characteristic or property of a body, that can be measured: the distance, the mass and the time interval, for example, are physical quantities. Whereas in Classical Mechanics any physical quantity is measurable (it is so represented by real functions or numbers), in Quantum Mechanics the physical quantities are represented by special functions named mathematical operators. Moreover, some physical quantities cannot be measured simultaneously, due to Heisenberg's uncertainty principle.

In Classical Mechanics for example, the position of a point particle moving on the straight line with constant acceleration is represented by the hourly law:

$$s(t) = s_0 + v_0 t + \frac{1}{2} a t^2$$

where $s(t)$ is the position at a precise instant of time t, s_0 and v_0 are the position and velocity at instant $t = 0 \ s$ and a is the acceleration of the point particle. This law is generally represented by a mathematical function named parabola, whose value $s(t)$ at an instant of time t is just the position of the point particle.

In Quantum Mechanics, the state of a system is defined by a set of vectors $|\psi\rangle$ on a mathematical space, named Hilbert space H. Observables such as position, velocity, angular momentum are associated with a mathematical operator that gives us the values (eigenvalues) that it can assume. If the state of a system has not yet been defined, then a physical quantity can assume, after a measurement procedure, a specific value with a certain probability. One peculiarity is that, in Quantum Mechanics, obtaining a certain value associated with a physical quantity is intrinsically probabilistic, and is not just a matter of knowledge, as in Classical Physics. As an example of this statement we could imagine a box with two balls inside, one of which is white, and the other blue. If we extract one ball, we have the probability equal to 50 percent that it is white or blue. Before the extraction procedure, the color of each ball is already defined within the box from the point of view of Classical Physics. In Quantum Mechanics, instead, the color of each ball doesn't exist until we extract it from the box: each ball is in a superposition of states of color (blue and white) and, only when we watch it, it will assume just one color, with a probability equal to 50 percent.

To understand the concept of superposition of states we give an example: when we hear a sound, we know that this sound is the superposition of several waves, each at its own acoustic frequency. The image of the spectrum of a sound gives us, moment by moment, the intensity of each wave that makes up that sound.

In Quantum Mechanics the state of a system is represented by the superposition of all possible states. So, if we want to talk, in general, about the position of a particle, the state that represents it is given by the sum of all the possible positions (each one with its own probability).

When we measure the position physical quantity, we get, as a result of the measurement, just one value between the allowed ones.

In Quantum Mechanics, the concept of superposition can also be extended to multiple particle systems. Given a couple of particles, for example, you can describe in a more general way a unique function for both their states instead of two separate functions. Such a quantum state is defined by the superposition of all possible states of both particles: one wave function describes the state of two particles. If the two particles are not related in any way, the probability of finding the first particle, for example, in the position x and the second particle the position y is given by the product of the two independent probabilities $P(x)$e $P(y)$:

$$P(x,y) = P(x)P(y).$$

If the two particles are entangled, the two wave functions and probabilities cannot be mathematically factorized; that is represented by the product of two functions. This means that the state of one particle cannot be fully described without considering the other. If we have two distinct particles that share the same wave function, a single measurement on one of the two causes the wave function to collapse for both, thus providing the value of the observable for both the particles.

Imagine now an experiment with two balls entangled in their colors; two experimenters, Alice and Bob, extract two balls from two boxes. Alice's and Bob's laboratories are spatially separated, and the two balls can be white and blue, after a measurement. As already stated, each ball is in a superposition state of colors that is white and blue, until somebody extracts them. Imagine also that each ball, when extracted, will just be of one specific color, due to some physical law (wave function collapse). Assume also that Alice first performs her measure, getting a white ball: when Bob extracts the ball from his box, he will surely obtain a blue one. One consequence of this fact is that, measuring an observable of one of these systems simultaneously involves the measurement of all the other observables; the wave function collapse will assign an eigenvalue to the color of each ball.

Jung states that:

> Since psyche and matter are contained in one and the same world, and moreover are in continuous contact with one another and ultimately rest on irrepresentable, transcendental factors, it is not only possible but fairly probable, even, that psyche and matter are two different aspects of the same thing.
>
> (*Collected Works 8*, Jung, 1960: 279)

This interpretation finds an analogy with quantum entanglement: different quantum systems turn out to be subsystems of just a wider one. Fleischer (2022) discusses the correspondence between body and psyche, referring to the story of one of her patients. Also in "The Origin and History of Embodied Active Imagination: Authentic Movement through the Life and Work of Its Early Pioneers; Chapter 2 of this volume), Fleischer discusses the evolution of active imagination in the somatic perspective that is Authentic Movement.

If we can make an analogy with the Jungian theory, the measurement itself represents the experience of the conscious Ego (the experimenter); an experience of the Ego in the psychic world could unveil a state not yet defined (the wave function collapse) in the matter realm.

In this sense, active imagination could be similar to quantum entanglement. Let's now return to the thought experiment carried out by Alice and Bob. We imagine that Alice and Bob share many couples of entangled balls, and that each ball could be of many colors; anyway some colors are coupled, meaning that, for example, if Alice obtains white, Bob will obtain blue with 100 percent certainty. Other couples of color could also be, for example, red and orange, brown and green, and so on; remember that, at this stage, Alice and Bob don't yet know the matching. Alice extracts a ball and obtains brown, for example; then she communicates the result of this measurement to Bob. Bob extracts a ball and obtains the color green, communicating it to Alice: now they both know that brown and green are coupled. In this way Alice and Bob, together, are able to add knowledge of their set of balls. This process is known in Physics as Quantum State Reconstruction. We cannot observe a quantum state, but we can reconstruct it by some observables that evolve according to this state.

In the parallel of active imagination, Alice represents the first two steps of the description given by Marie-Louise Von Franz, while Bob the latter two. Alice communicates Bob the result of her measurement, thus preparing the Ego to bring the inner experience into the physical world, where contents emerged from the unconscious come to life. In this way one could be able to couple together experiences from the psychic and from the physical world. The experimenter's action would be that of reuniting those apparently separated eigenvalues into a unique upper function. In this experience of acting in the two worlds, psychic and material, the Ego follows the path of Individuation, of Self-realization.

As concerns my personal experiences, I have often resorted to active imagination throughout my life, in different ways and for different reasons. One, in particular, that I would like to mention concerns the art to which I dedicate myself for a hobby; that is, painting. After having copied, for a long time, different subjects, such as people or still lives, I noticed that there was something in my paintings that concerns only me and exclusively me. I then wondered if I could study in depth this personal influence of mine, for example looking for images that were created exclusively in my unconscious, and for this reason I resorted to active imagination. During this practice, I have met characters and situations with whom I have interacted for the necessary time: looked at them, listened to and felt them. I also tried to remember images, feelings, sounds, that accompanied me during the phase of creations, when I painted these "dreams". As a result, the paintings that emerged showed somehow an action, as if life were flowing in them. Looking at these paintings is more like interacting with another world, watching from the window of the canvas, rather than looking at a picture. A similar work, developed in the field of music, is described in this book in Chapter 13, "*Intro-Spettro*: 64 Acousmatic Examples of Synchronicity" by G. Aiolli.

To summarize, in this chapter, I have presented an analogy between the practice of Active Imagination and Quantum State Reconstruction. In the latter, we measure the eigenvalues of different observables, with the aim of reconstructing a complete wave function; in the practice of active imagination, we work in parallel on the psychic and material planes, thus achieving Self-awareness. By associating with the Self, the complete wave function that evolves our existence, it is easy to see how the two processes can be somehow associated. Further investigation could be carried out into this analogy, while the purpose of this chapter was only to propose its existence.

References

Fleischer, K. (2022) "Collective trauma, implicit memories, the body, and active imagination in Jungian analysis", Congress Proceedings for *XXII International Congress for Analytical Psychology, August 28 to September 2, 2022, Buenos Aires, Argentina*. Daimon Verlag, Switzerland.

Jung, C.G. (1960) *Collected Works*, vol. 8, Princeton: Princeton University Press.

Jung, C.G. (1969) *Collected Works*, vol. 9, Princeton: Princeton University Press.

Jung, C.G. (1976) *Collected Works*, vol. 18, Princeton: Princeton University Press.

Meier, C.A. (2001) (Ed.) *Atom and Archetype, The Pauli/Jung Letters, 1932–1958*, Princeton and Oxford: Princeton University Press.

Von Franz, M.L. (1980) "On Active Imagination", in *Inward Journey: Art as Therapy*, 17 (La Salle and London: Open Court, 1983).

Chapter 13

Intro-Spettro

64 Acousmatic Examples of Synchronicity

Giacomo Aiolli

Introduction

Intro-Spettro is a musical work built through a series of cause–effect relationships managed by a stochastic algorithm. The idea for *Intro-Spettro* has its roots in the concept of Active Imagination proposed by Carl Gustav Jung. Active Imagination is one of the pillars of Jungian psychology and consists of giving form to the images of the unconscious and being able to dialogue with them. This method is based on focusing attention on emotions and, more generally, on unconscious contents brought to consciousness, letting them develop freely but interacting with them. I first came across this topic while I was working on the soundtrack of the documentary "The Lighting of Shadow Images – Interview with Giuseppe Tornatore",[1] where the author Chiara Tozzi asks the movie director Giuseppe Tornatore to share his thoughts on the four phases of Active Imagination in relation to his work. I quickly noticed that there were several points in common with my approach and realized that my creative moments were characterized by combinations of significant events and coincidences. I therefore tried to investigate the correlation between Active Imagination and Synchronicity to analyze my compositional approach in a deeper way.

C.G. Jung refers to synchronistic events as an "act of creation in time" (Jung, 1952/1969, paragraph 965): in fact the relationship between active imagination and synchronicity is very close, as underlined by Chiara Tozzi in her reference to the possibility of an attitude of Active Imagination in everyday life (Tozzi, forthcoming). The correlation between active imagination and synchronicity can also be referred to the example given by Murray Stein (2017) in which the matter of time is addressed through an active imagination of the Austrian physicist Wolfgang Pauli, where the dualism time/eternity is presented through "Pauli's World Clock", which Jung interpreted "as a symbol for the intersection of time and eternity, or 'real time' and 'imaginary time', to use more modern terminology".

Thus, I took inspiration from the *I Ching*, the Chinese philosophy whose interpretative mechanism consists in the combination of two types of lines in 64 different associations, to be able to create a composition that will develop and end in 64 different ways. I used the Active Imagination method to produce the sound

DOI: 10.4324/9781003411383-13

material in association with the *I Ching* basic elements (lines and trigrams); then I looked to the associations led by the random algorithm as synchronistic events and let myself be inspired by these solutions to compose the main core of every alternative. From the listener's point of view, *Intro-Spettro* is a work of consultative value since no one (even the author) will ever be able to predict which of the 64 possible paths will be taken by the algorithm, and the user will therefore be master and submissive at the same time, leaving him- or herself engaging emotionally or looking for a personal meaning – or response – in the music selected by the mechanism. My goal was to prove that we receive an infinite variety of impulses in our life and that our creative flow (but also our way of speaking and relating) is not a free movement but the result of a combination of pseudo-random events that lead us to produce an idea, to pronounce a particular word or to make some movement. What is the relationship between chance and causality? How much does chance affect our everyday life and, consequently, the human creative process? To find an answer to my questions, I initially needed to explore the fundamental principles of quantum mechanical physics, such as the principle of non-locality, quantum potential and the wave function.

Atomic Music

The Non-locality Phenomenon

Quantum mechanics can be considered one of the most important theories of modern science. It describes the behavior of matter in a completely different way compared to classical or Newtonian physics, based on the theories of Isaac Newton, the English physicist who considered light as a wave and electrons as particles; in quantum mechanics, conversely, matter and radiation are described as part of the same phenomenon (wave–particle dualism).

In the quantum paradigm, a particularly surprising aspect emerges: subatomic particles are able to communicate information to each other instantly, even if they are far apart; therefore they are connected in a non-local way.

The non-locality phenomenon appears for the first time in a famous article entitled "Can Quantum-Mechanical Description of Reality Be Considered Complete?", written by Einstein, Podolsky and Rosen (1935), but it founds his complete explanation in the article "On the Einstein-Podolski-Rosen Paradox" published in 1964 by the Irish physicist John Stewart Bell.

Wave Function

I mentioned above the wave–particle dualism; that is, the dual nature, both corpuscular and wave, of the behavior of matter. As Max Born hypothesized in 1927, an electron would be a probability wave; it would be "smeared" throughout the universe, with more and less dense points, and would be able to tell us how likely it is that the particle is in one point or another of space. In fact, assuming to take a sort of snapshot of a probability wave, we would have the wave function of the electron at that exact moment, or we would know the map of its probable positions.

But then will the position of the particle always be random? Not completely. The electron would be guided by a quantum "potential", theorized by David Bohm in the 1950s, which is able to deliver informations through non-local and simultaneous connections between quantum systems. According to Bohm, quantum potential informs each particle how and when to move, as if it were following a hidden plan that leads it to a universal cooperation.

Quantum Physics and Music

There is a strong connection between music and quantum mechanics: the scientific theories introduced in the last century have added concepts such as ambiguity and uncertainty in the way of observing the reality that surrounds us.

Just like quantum physics, musical language is based on the indeterminacy and on the overlapping of melodies which, unlike verbal language, allows simultaneous layers of meaning; for this reason, musical scores often present a symbolic language hard to decode, and even a single musical note gains meaning within a specific context. Examples such as French music between the 1800s and 1900s, where the composers, Debussy and Satie above all, use chords that don't resolve definitively, leaving a sense of harmonic uncertainty, demonstrate tonal ambiguity and instability, just as we can observe in the behavior of the particles in the quantum paradigm.

We can then understand how much music is interconnected with the basic concepts of quantum mechanics; as we will see better later, the method used to create the musical hexagrams of *Intro-Spettro* is ambiguous and uncertain too and it's based on the same concepts.

Synchronicity and *I Ching*

Significant Coincidences

Jungian Analytical Psychology is based on ("meaningful") relationships, associations and coincidences. Synchronicity is not an explanation but is, first of all, the attempt to give a name to all those empirical facts that suggest the existence of "significant coincidences".

Jung spent many years working on his ideas about "significant coincidences" and synchronicity; in 1948 he began an intensive correspondence with the physicist Wolfgang Pauli to share his thoughts on it, but it was only in 1952 that he spread his considerations in an article titled "Synchronicity: An Acausal Connecting Principle", included in a volume published with Pauli called *The Interpretation of Nature and the Psyche.*

In Jung's framework, synchronistic phenomena include telepathy, divination practices such as the *I Ching*, and even the interpretation of astrology. Thus random events full of meaning are marked by the alignment of an objective physical occurrence with a psychological experience. However, the authenticity of these events is often questioned, as they are rare and exceptional, but their age-old tradition and the personal experiences of individuals are a shield.

Synchronicity and Music

Synchronicity is a recurring theme that many artists have faced throughout their creative processes. There are many examples of music inspired by Jung's research, just think of "In C" (1964) by Terry Riley, where every musician could decide when to play a specific measure creating a new piece at every performance, or the album *Synchronicity* (1983) by The Police, which contains many references to this theme.

In 1951 John Cage used the *Book of Changes* to create his composition *Music of Changes* (1951), an aleatory work in which the American composer relies on a square of 64 × 64 cells to make musical choices: every cell contains a value and through some random mechanism a computer chooses one of these possibilities. The approach to Eastern philosophies leads Cage towards the denial of the ego, the renunciation of expression and communication and the abandonment of human control over nature and sound, and his aleatory techniques are a way to imitate the way nature works.

The *Book of Changes*

The *I Ching*, or *Book of Changes*, is one of the oldest and most enigmatic books in the world. For more than 2,000 years it has been used in the East as a divination book, and nowadays is still studied with respectful deference as the source of Confucian and Taoist wisdom.

The *Book of Changes* includes a list of 64 hexagrams with their own traditional Chinese name and meaning; these symbols are the result of every possible permutation of two types of lines, taken six at a time. The two variations of lines signify the fundamental duality in Chinese metaphysics: the broken line embodies the concept of yin; the continuous line corresponds to yang. By considering three lines concurrently, there are eight (2 × 2 × 2) potential combinations for forming trigrams; by combining these eight, a total of 64 hexagrams are generated (8 × 8).

The *Book of Changes* can be consulted with the original method of the yarrow stalks or with one of the three coins, which is the one that I chose to represent in my work.

Three identical coins are taken, with one side designated as Yang (representing heads) and is worth 3, while the other (tails) is Yin and is worth 2. Following this setup, the coins are tossed at the same time. There are four possible combinations:

2 + 2 + 2 = 6, which gives mobile broken line, marked with "-x-"
3 + 2 + 2 = 7, which gives fixed broken line, marked with "—"

3 + 3 + 2 = 8, which gives fixed continuous line, marked with "- -"
3 + 3 + 3 = 9, which gives a mobile continuous line, marked with "-0-"

This operation is repeated six times, noting the single results gradually, starting from the bottom: in this way we will obtain one of the 64 hexagrams.

For *Intro-Spettro* I decided to reduce it to a single coin because for the purpose of my research it was enough to consider two types of line (broken and continuous).

Inside the Work

Strategy

My idea was to develop a sound object which, starting from a creative cue, would then be used as a source of inspiration, creating some kind of "compositional domino effect".

I structured my work by determining that the sequence of selected events started from an elementary object and ended up with more and more layered sound objects over time. In fact, it was my intention to demonstrate how a system based on a simple continuous/broken dualism can generate a system that becomes more and more complex. After all, just like a multicellular organism formed over time, even an artistic work can represent an example of evolution, since the artist only applies choices to the various alternatives that are presented to him or her, in a crescendo of combinations and associations of meaning.

To create and organize my 64 compositions in *Intro-Spettro*, I used Logic Pro X, a digital audio workstation, and Max MSP, an interactive graphic environment for music, audio and multimedia.

Project

I took inspiration from the consultation mechanism of the *Book of Changes* to create a hybrid system that would allow me to identify a gray area between randomness and causality. I therefore decided to program an algorithm capable of simulating the coin toss and the construction of hexagrams, and to manage "randomly" the sound associations I had prepared using Max MSP.

I created a patch on Max MSP, starting from the formulation of the coin toss; I used the "random" object to make the computer choose one of two possible results (heads or tails), reduced to 0 and 1. Depending on the result obtained, one of the two sound sequences is activated (see the "Development" and "Production" sections) associated with the first of the six levels of the hexagram. This process is repeated five more times thanks to the "counter" object, until it stops thanks to the deactivation of the "toggle" object (the one that started the "counter"). The same values used to select the initial sequences will also be addressed to two matrices that will represent the two resulting trigrams. Each point of the matrix will light up if it receives the value 1 (broken line) and will remain off if reached by the value 0, thus also composing the two trigrams graphically.

Subsequently, thanks to the "unpack" and "accum" objects, I made some operations on the values that matrices eject from their "output" to differentiate each of the eight possible results (1, 3, 4, 5, 6, 7, 8, 10). With these integer values, the two "playlist" objects are able to select the sound sample associated with that trigram.

Finally, I transformed the 16 values received (8 × 2) into prime numbers since they are numbers that if multiplied together always generate different results. By setting each resulting product to a value between 1 to 64, we will get the number that will activate the last section of the composition, which is different for every hexagram.

Development

Initially I associated two sound objects to each of the six possible lines of the hexagram, one perpetual if the line is continuous, and one intermittent if the line is broken.

Then, inspired by the sum of the three selected sound objects, I associated to every possible trigram (which in Chinese philosophy correspond to natural elements) two sound samples with similar sounds; the first to be activated when the trigram is in the lower position, the second in cases where it is in the upper position.

At this point, listening to the 64 possible pairs of trigrams, I independently composed a conclusive development inspired both by the sound atmospheres produced by the previous associations, and by the ancient oriental meaning of the resulting hexagram.

Production

I organized the work in three stages:

1. In the first one, I created 12 sound objects (6 continuous and 6 point-like) from which 6 will be selected by the algorithm in Max MSP.
2. In the second, I chose 16 soundscapes and associated them with the 16 possible trigrams (8 in the upper position and the same 8 in the lower position).
3. In the third stage, I composed a music inspired by the associations selected by the algorithm.

Thus, each of the 64 compositions will be divided into two macro-sections:

1. In the first section, we will see the gradual construction of a layered sound system, starting from simple elements (a continuous sine wave or a sequence of sinusoidal impulses) up to richer and more complex textures and rhythms. So in the first minute of each composition, we will often find recurring elements since, for example, there are four trigrams starting with a broken line, eight hexagrams with the trigram "mount" in the lower position and eight others with the same

trigram in the upper position (earth ☷ and sky ☰, for example, will not have any sound element in common since they didn't share any kind of line).
2. In the second section, the composition will take its own direction, since the sum of the elements selected by the algorithm will slowly turn into a unique entity, despite the strong connection with the previous atmospheres, which will be inspired by the sounds originating from the initial associations.

The Soul's Spectrum

I have always thought that a human's personality is multiple and indefinable, and that it's impossible to understand and control it completely.

As the wave function of the quantum paradigm is concentrated in one point only when observed, every human's personality will take its real shape depending on the situation. So, we can assume a certain behavior and we can say a specific word for multiple reasons, but we need to remember that we are beings in a state of constant change and that the word we have chosen at a specific time could be another one a second later. Just as there are points in the particle's wave function where the chance to find it is more concentrated, human personality is also affected by growth experiences and the surrounding environment; however, this does not prevent thought and personality from changing in an apparently random way.

Intro-Spettro acts as a "medium" for an evocative consultation that works as a stimulus, a source of inspiration or simply a meditative break. At last, each listener is called to seek their own personal approach for consulting the algorithm, since the structure of the piece was created specifically fluid and variable.

The listener can ask him- or herself a question, make a wish, or simply clear his or her mind and accept one of the 64 possible ways without preconceptions, taking up the Jungian attitude of Active Imagination, the attitude in everyday life mentioned earlier (Tozzi, forthcoming).

64 Possible Significant Coincidences

The listener has no control over the final result of *Intro-Spettro*'s associative mechanism: he or she can only press the start button. The action of pressing the right mouse button and starting the associations can be mistaken for an irrelevant action: but if the button had been pressed a microsecond earlier, what would be the result? We'll never know, but this question allows us to understand the importance of the relationship between space, time and coincidences (especially the significant ones). How many opportunities have we lost for a moment, sometimes without even knowing it?

For these reasons, in my opinion, it is important to take a deep breath and concentrate before pressing start. *Intro-Spettro* is a composition (the one resulting at that moment for the listener) but, until the start button is pressed, it will be the sum of all the 64 compositions present in the algorithm playlists.

Conclusion

Quantum mechanics has told us that some kind of law lies in our universe, which is not perceptible to our senses; in the same way, in the micro-universe I created for this work, my intervention is active and arbitrary, since I established rules.

Anyway, the 64 tracks will have their own development and will range from electroacoustic music, more experimental, to ambient music, more melodic, creating a sort of spectrum containing 64 different shades of my influences and creativity, all originating from significant coincidences produced by the algorithm, which were a spark for my inspiration. *Intro-Spettro* will therefore be simultaneously all 64 compositions present in the algorithm's playlists, just as an electron will have both negative and positive spin until the time of its observation. By assigning the decision-making power to the algorithm, I tried to reduce human intervention to emphasize the importance of chance and significant coincidences in our life, and in creative production too.

Intro-Spettro, just like Active Imagination, has been a way to receive, animate, meet and represent my images and contents that emerged from the unconscious (in this case, my inner music) and I hope that listeners can be inspired by this work to find their own.

For further details, check this link:

https://soundcloud.com/fantomatic-cangaru/sets/intro-spettro/s-4g9WV3Uxi W4?utm_source=clipboard&utm_medium=text&utm_campaign=social_sharing

By connecting to this link, everyone will discover four examples of hexagrams. Additionally, they will find an email address to which they can write to experience this method and to consult personally this musical *I Ching*.

Note

1 "The lighting of shadow images – Interview with Giuseppe Tornatore", by Chara Tozzi, screened at the IAAP Film and Analytical Psychology Conference, Belgrade, June 2023.

References

Bell, J.S. (1964). "On the Einstein-Podolsky-Rosen paradox", *Physics*, 1: 195–200.
Born, M. (1927). *Mechanics of the Atom*. Translated by J.W. Fisher and revised by D.R. Hartree, Bell.
Cipriani, A. and Girim, M. (2009). "Electronic music and sound design", ConTempoNet.
Einstein, A., Podolsky, B. and Rosen, N. (1935). "Can quantum-mechanical description of physical reality be considered complete?" *Physical Review*, 47: 777.
Greene, B. (2004). *La trama del cosmo*, Einaudi.
Jung, C.G. (1952/1969) "Synchronicity: An Acausal connecting principle", in H. Read, M. Fordham, G. Adler (eds), *The Structure and Dynamics of the Psyche, The Collected Works of C.G. Jung*, vol. 8, Princeton: Princeton University Press.

Jung, C.G. (1980). *Synchronicity*, Bollati Boringhieri.

Jung, C.G. and Pauli, W. ([1952]1922). *The Interpretation of Nature and the Psyche*. London and New York: Routledge.

Li Vigni, A. (2014). "Musicalità atomica", *Il sole 24 ore*, April 13.

Roads, C. (1995). *The Computer Music Tutorial*, MIT press.

Stein, M. (2017). *Synchronizing Time and Eternity: A Matter of Practice*, Chiron Pub.

Tozzi, C. (2023) "Active Imagination and Testament: A window on the other side of life", in *Individuation Psychology: Essays in Honor of Murray Stein*, Chiron.

Wilhelm, R. (1967) The I Ching or Book of Changes (with preface by C.G.Jung), Princeton University Press, 3rd edition Adelphi.

Index

Please note that page references to Figures will be in **bold**. Footnotes will be denoted by the letter 'n' and Note number following the page number.

For Product Safety Concerns and Information please contact our EU
representative GPSR@taylorandfrancis.com
Taylor & Francis Verlag GmbH, Kaufingerstraße 24, 80331 München, Germany

www.ingramcontent.com/pod-product-compliance
Lightning Source LLC
Chambersburg PA
CBHW050613280326
41932CB00016B/3029

9 781032 533025